How to Develop Your Thinking Ability

Kenneth S. Keyes, Jr.

Illustrated by Ted Key

McGraw-Hill Book Company, Inc.
New York Toronto London

HOW TO DEVELOP YOUR THINKING ABILITY

Published by the McGraw-Hill Book Company, Inc.

Printed in the United States of America

First McGraw-Hill Paperback Edition, 1963

11 12 13 - MUMU - 7 5

ISBN 07-034461-2

To Roberta,
whose love and devotion have been
a constant source of encouragement and strength,
and without whose help as wife, adviser, and scribe,
this book would never have been written

THINKING ABOUT THINKING

Ludwig was just getting back from a three months' course of instruction at a school for stutterers.

"How was it? Did it help you?" asked his friend who met him at the station.

"Peter Piper picked a peck of pickled peppers," said Ludwig with nonchalant ease.

"Why, that's wonderful! I can't even do that myself."

"Yes, b-but but it's d-d-darn hard to w-work into an ordinary c-c-conversation."

This book doesn't contain a lot of impractical Peter Piper advice on how to develop your thinking ability. In it you will find ideas and techniques you can use right away in solving your minute-to-minute everyday problems. It explains the most fascinating, interesting, and important thing in your life: how to get the best results out of that wonderful brain you have been given—and about whose efficient operation you probably know less than you know about the engine of your car.

A friend of mine, Daniel Crowley of Peoria, Illinois, was waiting for his discharge at the U.S. Naval Hospital in Charleston, South Carolina. One day a Navy attendant asked:

"What are you reading?"

"This is a book on how we can make the most of our

mental powers," replied Crowley. "It tells how to think straight."

"What the hell?" said the attendant with evident disgust. "Who wants to think straight?"

When Crowley wrote me of this dissenting opinion, I was about half finished with this book. I was nonplused, if not shocked. I had assumed that people in general wanted to think clearly; I was hoping that millions were waiting to read my book. Could this sailor be right?

So I decided I had better do some checking. During the next year, I conducted a most unscientific, undefinitive (but, I think, interesting) survey of public opinion with the following questions:

1. Which of the following would you most hate to have people say about you?

   a. You do not win friends easily.
   b. You cannot think clearly.
   c. You have trouble influencing people.
   d. One day your pants fell down when your arms were loaded with packages.

2. Why did you make that choice?

This nation-wide survey revealed that of all the people who filled out and sent in the questionnaire, 72½ per cent thought it most important to be known as a clear thinker. A total of 19 per cent reported they would most hate to be known as one who does not win friends easily, and less than 2 per cent said they most feared a reputation for having trouble influencing people. I was surprised to find that the opinion of

6½ per cent was that sartorial security was most important.

Here are some of the reasons I received explaining why people believe it is so important to develop one's thinking ability:

1. Men and women who think clearly can achieve greater popularity. They are looked up to; their ideas are considered "worth listening to"; they are invited to analyze the ideas and plans of other people.
2. Women agree that they prefer to marry a man who stands out from the crowd in his thinking ability.
3. Men agree that they prefer women who are reasonable instead of emotional in meeting the problems of everyday life.
4. The ability to think clearly and maturely is an important step in the avoidance of worry and unhappiness . . . and the achievement of peace of mind.
5. In general, people agreed that clear thinking would automatically help them to win friends and influence people, and no doubt assist in making pants behave, too.

What This Book Will Do for You

The first ten chapters explain clearly the most effective system known for developing your thinking ability. The last five chapters show you how this simple system for straight thinking will help you to:

1. Get along better with other people.
2. Build a happier marriage.
3. Be successful in business.

4. Find causes for things that worry you.
5. Do your part to build a world free from war and want.

Our brains, like our bodies, don't come with a set of directions attached. And most of us stumble on through life without getting a very good set of "Directions for Use." This book was written to enable you to step up your ability to turn out sound decisions. When you use these easily understood techniques, you will find a remarkable increase in your capacity to think straight. And you won't need to tell your friends about it —they will notice.

Even a quick glance at this scrambled world should convince anyone that teachable methods for straight thinking are long overdue. To make this book interesting and profitable to everyone, regardless of his educational background, it has been necessary to drop overboard the usual technical terms, philosophical tangleweeds, and academic style. You will find it as practical as a five-dollar bill. And if you train yourself to apply these simple techniques for straight thinking, you will obtain benefits and rewards worth hundreds of five-dollar bills.

ACKNOWLEDGMENTS

First of all, I wish to acknowledge my great debt to the late Alfred Korzybski, the formulator of the science of general semantics whose work has been the inspiration for this book.

I also want to express my appreciation of the help I have received from the writings of others who have explored the field of scientific thinking. Those to whom I am especially indebted are Edwin Leavitt Clarke, Morris R. Cohen, John Dewey, S. I. Hayakawa, Wendell Johnson, Harold A. Larrabee, Irving J. Lee, William A. McCall, and Karl Pearson.

I particularly thank Dr. William McCall of Teachers College, Columbia, for his careful reading and criticism. I am also happy to record my thanks to the following individuals who have given me the benefit of their reactions to the manuscript:

H. Briscoe Black, Kathleen Bushey, Reverend Richard E. Hanson, Ann Kinder-Jones, Henry and Sylvia Lieferant, Guthrie and Gila Jansen, Graham C. Miller, and Dr. and Mrs. John E. Walker.

I wish to express my appreciation to Ted Key for his sympathetic and effective interpretation of this book as expressed in his cartoons.

Many thanks are due to Lucille T. Keyes, Kenneth S. Keyes, Sr., Clara D. Rymer, and S. B. Rymer, Sr., for their kind encouragement and assistance.

I am grateful to the authors and publishers who have given permission to reprint from their publications. Individual acknowledgments have been made in the text by footnotes.

KENNETH S. KEYES, JR.

CONTENTS

Part III

USING THE TOOLS IN EVERYDAY LIFE

Part I

WHAT IS STRAIGHT THINKING?

I

Your Verbal Maps

What is straight thinking? What will it do for you?

Straight thinking will tend to make your foresight as good as your hindsight. Clear thinking helps you to predict the future. It enables you to make plans that will get you what you want out of life.

Suppose you are starting out on a week-end trip to your favorite lake. You get one of the latest road maps and pick the best-looking route. But when you are a little beyond Plankerville, you find that road repairs make you detour through thirty miles of the dustiest dirt road you've ever breathed. You feel hot and grimy, and the polish job on the car is shot.

Why did you get fouled up? *The map on which you relied did not represent the territory adequately.* Last week it may have represented the territory quite well, but that does not help get the dust out of your ears NOW. At the time you used it, your map lacked *predictability.*

Whenever you use maps that do not adequately represent the territory—maps that have poor predictability—you will not

A MAP SHOULD REPRESENT THE TERRITORY

If a map does not *adequately* represent the territory, we cannot make reliable predictions from it.

get what you want. Bad maps will lead you to anything from minor annoyance to sudden death, depending upon the nature of the situation.

One of the best ways to understand the problem of straight thinking is to think in terms of maps. Throughout this book we're going to use the term VERBAL MAP, so let's get acquainted with it right now.

A verbal map is simply a map or a "picture" drawn with words.

A reliable VERBAL MAP represents the territory adequately; a bad VERBAL MAP lies to you about the territory.

For example, if I say, "Mosquitoes breed in standing water," I have made a verbal map that represents the territory. If someone tells you, "Female canaries sing," he has given you an incorrect map that will mislead you if you rely upon it.

Every time you open your mouth to let out words, you are making a VERBAL MAP. If you tell Junior "George Washington was the first President of the United States," you are making a map of territory that existed over a century ago. If Henry Brown says, "Beginning next year, I will definitely cut out smoking," he is making a VERBAL MAP of future territory. If he stops smoking, as the map says, it represents the actual territory. Otherwise, no. When I say, "My big toe hurts," I am making a VERBAL MAP of some territory that I, alone, am able to survey. I am mapping territory within my own body. If I say, "I am very disappointed," I am again mapping territory within me—my feelings.

All the knowledge and memories we have filed away in our heads may be regarded as "mental maps." All the thousands of words we shoot at each other every day may be regarded

"But I never really loved anyone but you."

as verbal maps representing past, present, or future territory.

The problem of straight thinking is: DO MY VERBAL MAPS ADEQUATELY REPRESENT THE TERRITORY? If THEY DO, I CAN RELY ON THEM. I CAN PREDICT FROM THEM. MY PLANS WILL WORK. IF MY VERBAL MAPS DO NOT REPRESENT THE TERRITORY, TROUBLE LURKS AHEAD.

Inadequate Maps Put Us in Hot Water

Tim McCarthy was hit by a truck, and the first report of the doctor was discouraging. "I'm afraid your husband hasn't long to live," he told Tim's wife. "I'll come again tomorrow.'

The next day, the doctor's report was still gloomy. But when the doctor called a third time, the patient was rallying, and on the fourth day he was out of danger.

"Well, missus," the doctor said. "Tim is going to pull through all right."

"Puts me in a bit of a hole, though," said the woman. "I've gone and sold all his clothes for funeral expenses."

Whenever we act on maps that do not adequately represent the territory, it puts us in a "bit of a hole."

In everything we do, we need adequate verbal maps. If we make a mistake in our checking account and think the balance is $352 when it is only $241.50, some of our checks are going to bounce. The map in our checkbook must adequately represent the funds in our account if we are to avoid trouble. If the gas gauge in our car says half full when our tank is about empty, it does not map the territory very well. If we rely on it, our blood pressure is going up—especially if we want to get somewhere in a hurry.

Don't Buy That Map

Some people find it profitable to mislead us with inaccurate verbal maps. A house hunter, who had just got off a train, said to a boy near the station:

"Son, I'm looking for Mr. Wilson's new block of semi-detached cottages. How far are they from here?"

"About twenty minutes' walk."

"Twenty minutes!" exclaimed the house hunter. "Nonsense, the advertisement says only five."

"Well," drawled the boy. "You can believe me, or you can believe the ad, but I ain't tryin' to make a sale."

The disappointing sagas of quack medicines, miraculous toothpastes that clean our teeth by grinding off enamel, confidence and skin games, phony get-rich-quick schemes, lost manhood cures, and the gasoline-mileage car salesmen claim all warn us that, if we want to avoid disappointment, we must inquire closely into the reliability of the verbal maps people give us.

Some men were gathered around the stove in the village store discussing the way farmer Silas Perkins was so economical with the truth. At the end of the discussion his next-door neighbor spoke up:

"Well, maybe Si ain't such an awful liar, but around our way when feeding time comes, he has to get someone else to call his hogs for him!"

Even animals want maps that represent the territory! To enjoy the confidence of animals or human beings, we must make maps that jibe with the actual territory. A liar is not believed even when he tells the truth. And the truth can be described simply as a verbal map that represents the territory.

WE GET INTO TROUBLE WHEN OUR VERBAL MAPS DON'T REPRESENT THE TERRITORY

"Guess that python wasn't so sick after all."

Use the Term "Verbal Map" in Your Thinking

"If we reflect upon our languages," wrote Alfred Korzybski in his famous work *Science and Sanity,* "we find that at best they must be considered *only as maps.*" * We are going to cut through a lot of scholarly underbrush by describing straight thinking as simply making maps that adequately represent the territory. As you get into this book, you will see what a useful approach this is. Begin right now to use the idea of the VERBAL MAP in your thinking.

Instead of saying, "Now, Junior, tell the truth," say, "Now, Junior, make your maps represent the territory."

At the office, you can say to yourself, "When I make that report to the boss on what our competitors are doing, my verbal maps must adequately represent the territory. Otherwise, we can't plan effectively."

At home, you might say, "The verbal maps given me by the garbage man were lousy. He said he would be here Tuesday. Now it's Wednesday afternoon and the can is so full the top won't go on."

When we actually begin to think in terms of making ADEQUATE VERBAL MAPS, it will be much easier for us to apply the principles set forth in this book. You will be surprised at how much the simple idea of verbal mapping can help you, once you have used it enough to explore its possibilities.

Why Accurate Maps May Not Be Good Enough

You may have wondered why so much emphasis has been put upon "ADEQUATE" verbal maps. The word "adequate"

* Reprinted by permission. Copyright, 1933, 1941, 1948, by Alfred Korzybski.

has been carefully chosen. A verbal map may be considered strictly accurate and yet, *for our purposes,* be quite inadequate and misleading!

For example, Bob had fished all day without any luck. On his way home he went to Captain Tom's Fish Market and said:

"Tom, pick out five of your biggest fish and toss them to me."

"You mean throw them?"

"Yes, just throw them over to me one at a time so I can tell the family I caught them. I may be a poor fisherman, but I'm no liar."

Some people might say our fisherman was making an "accurate" verbal map if he said he caught the fish. But no one would insisit it was an ADEQUATE verbal map. We see readily that however accurate that map is, it is thoroughly misleading and has nothing to do with the actual territory.

Often, we call such things "white lies." Now I'm not saying that an occasional white lie isn't useful when our sweetheart asks us how we like her new hat. Tact and courtesy sometimes dictate that the map should not represent the actual territory. But when it comes to important decisions—when it comes to getting along in this complex world of ours—we must have adequate verbal maps if we are to get what we want. Our happiness and our success depend almost entirely upon the ADEQUACY of the maps we make in our personal, social, and business affairs.

Here is an *accurate* verbal map of someone we all know about:

Mr. A. H. had an unhappy childhood and little formal edu-

WE NEED MAPS THAT ADEQUATELY REPRESENT THE TERRITORY

"And *you* said he was a gentleman."

cation. His ambition to become an artist was bitterly opposed by his father. Although self-educated, he became the author of a book, the sales of which in his country ranked next to the Bible. Obstacles did not discourage him. People would say, "Why, you can't do that!" but he hurdled one barrier after another. He placed a great deal of emphasis upon improving the health of young people, and he was known throughout the world as a dynamic speaker. His closest associate said of him: "[He] accomplishes great deeds out of the greatness of his heart, the passion of his will, and the goodness of his soul."

Sounds like a pretty good man, doesn't he? **So far as I know,** everything in the foregoing description of *Adolf Hitler* is accurate and verifiable. . . . Notice how we can be woefully misled by an accurate map! Only an ADEQUATE, well-rounded, balanced map deserves our trust. An adequate map is accurate, but an accurate map is not necessarily ADEQUATE. We must avoid mistaking one for the other.

What to Expect from This Book

"Life," remarked Kierkegaard, "can only be understood backwards; but it must be lived forwards."

Every chapter in this book has been written with one dominant purpose: *to show you habits of thinking that will help you make adequate verbal maps.*

You may find that you now have many thinking habits that make it difficult *and sometimes impossible* for you to make adequate verbal maps that will serve you well in your everyday life situations. But, as you get into this book, you will discover some efficient methods *that can double or triple your present skill in making adequate verbal maps.*

To Sum Up

Clear thinking simply means making adequate verbal maps. To be happy and successful, we must base our plans on maps that fit the territory. Only an adequate map will have the necessary predictability that will allow us to plan, to choose, to decide what is best for us to do.

When you first meet the notion of VERBAL MAPPING, it will naturally seem strange and unfamiliar. But once you learn to use it, you will find it a fruitful approach to the problem of straight thinking.

2

Surveying the Territory

One look is worth one hundred reports
JAPANESE PROVERB

A dictator was telling a group about the marvelous accomplishments under his rule. In glowing terms he described the new twenty-story skyscrapers.

"But sir," spoke up an old man in the audience, "I've lived here for the last fifty years. At night after supper I walk with my wife and children and we've never seen the skyscrapers. . . ."

"That's the trouble with you," the dictator interrupted angrily. "You waste your time walking the streets instead of reading the newspapers and finding out what is going on in your country."

How do we get our verbal maps? We have a choice: firsthand or secondhand. We can survey the territory ourselves and make our own verbal maps. Or we can read or talk to other people and get our maps secondhand.

BEWARE OF SECONDHAND MAPS

"It is reliably re-
ported in official
circles today...."

Some of the time we get into trouble because we do not take advantage of the experiences of other people; we don't profit by the wisdom of the "old-timers." But most of us have developed quite well the habit of using secondhand verbal maps—of relying on the knowledge and experiences of other people. We have acquired this habit so well that we have become lax in the practice of surveying the territory ourselves and making our own verbal maps. This chapter (and this entire book) will help you develop to a greater extent the ability *and habit* of making your own verbal maps.

The Limitations of Maps

"I visited the troops near Coutances on the twenty-ninth," wrote General George Patton, "and found an armored division sitting on a road, while its Headquarters, secreted behind an old church, was deeply engrossed in the study of maps. I asked why they had not crossed the Sienne. They told me they were making a study of it at the moment, but could not find a place where it could be forded. I asked what effort they had made to find such a place and was informed that they were studying the map to that end. I then told them I had just waded across it, that it was not over two feet deep, and that the only defense I knew about was one machine gun which had fired very inaccurately at me. I repeated the Japanese proverb: 'One look is worth one hundred reports,' and asked them why in hell they had not gone down to the river personally. They learned the lesson and from then on were a very great division." *

* From *War As I Knew It* by General George S. Patton, Jr. Boston: Houghton Mifflin Company. Copyright, 1947, by Beatrice Patton Waters, Ruth Patton Totten, and George Smith Patton. Reprinted by permission.

DON'T GO BLINDLY BY SECONDHAND MAPS;
USE YOUR OWN EYES

". . . and as my wife was saying—he's really a quiet little boy—
easy to manage, sensitive, unspoiled. . . ."

As Patton pointed out, maps may be a poor substitute for actually surveying the territory for ourselves. Patton did not criticize the map the division leader was using—those maps were probably accurate and quite adequate as far as they went. *Patton criticized his failure to supplement the map with his own observations.*

When You Have to Do It

Most of the time we don't have the opportunity to survey the territory for ourselves. We just *have* to rely upon the maps of others. For instance, we know from history books that Columbus began the tourist service to America in 1492. You and I can't map this territory for ourselves. It took place hundreds of years before we were born, and we must accept the maps of other people whom we believe are qualified to inform us reliably.

When a skilled mechanic in whom I have confidence tells me my car needs new piston rings, there is a limit to how far I care to poke my head inside the engine to check on his verbal map. If you tell me that the Sharpo razor blades are the dullest things you've seen, I probably won't insist on trying them out for myself. If you inform me that the food at the Dew Drop Inn is awful and the service even worse, I'll plan to eat somewhere else tonight.

When we think it worth while to rely on the verbal maps of another person, we should pick someone who is well qualified to advise us. If it is an important matter, we might check his verbal maps with those of others whom we consider equally well qualified. We should remember that not even the greatest authority in any field dealing with practical matters is always

SURVEY THE TERRITORY YOURSELF INSTEAD OF ASSUMING OR GUESSING

right. Authorities are people who are on the beam most of the time, or at least more often than the average person. But they are human beings and, like all other human beings, at times authorities have been wrong and will continue to be wrong. Columbus, Robert Fulton, Thomas Edison, the Wright brothers, and many others you can name accomplished things that the authorities said were impossible. And today *more than ever before* great achievements await those who have the patience and guts to investigate things the authorities now take for granted.

Remember that no one has yet found the net with which to ensnare truth once and for all. Truth is an elusive sprite that is hard to keep penned up.

We Must Use Our Own Sense and Senses

In our everyday business and personal affairs, we are dealing, usually, with things we can check for ourselves. But most of us have become so used to relying on the verbal maps of others that we have lost the precious habit of seeking firsthand knowledge.

During our school days, we get used to soaking up secondhand verbal maps in order to spout them out at examination time. John Dewey, one of our leading philosophers and educators, wrote as long ago as 1898:

> The famous complaint of Agassiz, that students could not see for themselves, is still repeated by every teacher of science in our high schools and colleges. How many teachers of science will tell you, for example, that, when their students are instructed to find out something about an object, their first demand is for a book in which they can read about it; their first

"He must be asleep—it's quiet upstairs."

> reaction, one of helplessness, when they are told that they must go to the object itself and let it tell its own story? It is not exaggerating to say that the book habit is so firmly fixed that very many pupils, otherwise intelligent, have a positive aversion to directing their attention to things themselves,—it seems so much simpler to occupy the mind with what someone else has said about these things. While it is mere stupidity not to make judicious use of the discoveries and attainments of others, the substitution of the seeing of others for the use of one's own eyes is such a self-contradictory principle as to require no criticism. We only need recognize the extent to which it actually obtains.*

Of course, all of us have some tendency toward surveying the territory for ourselves. Try putting up a "Wet Paint" sign and notice the response! For some reason or other, a "Wet Paint" sign seems to arouse a strong "I'm-going-to-see-for-myself" impulse. But when it comes to important business and personal matters, frequently we get into serious trouble because we do not use our own firsthand observations to check the secondhand maps we've picked up over the years.

Think of some of the mistakes you have made. Almost every one is due to going by maps that do not adequately represent the territory. How often could you have "stayed out of hot water" if you had gone to the trouble of surveying the territory yourself instead of depending on what someone else told you, or on your own guesses? Perhaps one-half of the time? For each person the answer will be different. You must decide for yourself **up to what point** you need to develop more of the "I'm from Missouri—you've got to show me" attitude.

* From *Education Today* by John Dewey. New York: G. P. Putnam's Sons. Courtesy of the publisher.

INFERENCES MUST BE CHECKED AGAINST THE TERRITORY

The Scientific Spirit

In January, 1941, some Michigan conservation officers found a hunter busily engaged in tearing down a sign just put up on a post in the forest. They asked the hunter if he knew what he was doing.

"Sure," he replied angrily. "I'm tearing down these signs that say a man can't hunt on land bought by the Conservation Department."

"Did you actually read the sign?" asked an officer.

"Well, I'll be darned!" the hunter exclaimed disgustedly, as he looked up *and saw* the lettering.

"HUNTING PERMITTED," the sign read.

No matter how much intelligence we may have, it is subject to a 50 to 100 per cent discount if we don't have the habit of basing our maps on a careful survey of the territory. Aristotle, one of the greatest intellects of ancient Greece, wrote that there were eight legs on a fly. Any fool could have corrected him by using his eyes and counting the six legs on a fly. And Aristotle was called "The Master of Those Who Know!" The learned Pliny said that at the approach of a menstruating woman, seeds would become sterile, plants would become parched, and the fruit would drop from the trees. Her very glance would dim mirrors, blunt knives, kill bees, and cause brass and iron to rust.

Throughout this chapter we have repeatedly emphasized this point: the best way to make adequate verbal maps is to survey the territory for yourself. To use your own sense and senses. TO OBSERVE.

A MAP IS NOT A COMPLETE SUBSTITUTE FOR USING YOUR OWN EYES

"We're safe now. The book says this species cannot climb."

But isn't that what scientists tell us to do? Is it not by adequately surveying the territory that scientists achieve the remarkable predictability that characterizes their verbal maps? *In fact, isn't surveying the territory the essence of the scientific method?*

When a scientist tries to find out which verbal map is the most adequate, he looks at the territory. He observes; he uses his senses; he opens his mind and his eyes. Nonscientific people try to settle problems by arguments and by armchair reasoning. For example, the scientific way to tell whether a cake tastes good is to eat it. The philosophical way is to analyze the recipe and psychoanalyze the cook—that is, do any and everything except actually survey the territory by tasting the cake.

You will find that the six **tools for thinking** presented in Part II of this book offer you the easiest and most effective way that has yet been found to develop the scientific spirit in meeting your everyday life problems. In fact, when you learn to use these **tools for thinking,** you won't have to *try* to develop a scientific spirit—*you'll automatically have it.* Before you know it, the scientific way of thinking (which is the most effective technique for straight thinking known to man) will be giving you surprising and unexpected power in solving your personal and business problems.

To Sum Up

"Men are apt to be much more influenced by words," said Pavlov, "than by the actual facts of the surrounding reality."

The habit of surveying the territory for ourselves helps us get the words out of our eyes. It keeps us from developing

ADEQUATE MAPS ARE MADE BY SURVEYING THE TERRITORY

"You can almost always tell what a man does by looking at him. Take those two. Man near the window probably a professor or doctor or professional man. . . ."

"Excuse me, I know this request sounds strange, but my wife and I were just discussing. . . ."

a parasitic mind that lives on secondhand maps made by others.

The scientific way of making adequate verbal maps is to look at the territory instead of burying our nose too deeply in the reports of others. Once we learn to use the **six tools for thinking** (presented fully in Part II), we will find that we have automatically acquired a scientific attitude in dealing with our everyday affairs.

3

How to Get the Most Out of This Book

All truly wise thoughts have been thought already thousands of times; but to make them truly ours, we must think them over again honestly, till they take root in our personal experience.

GOETHE

Education has been described as the only thing people will pay for and yet refuse to get. Most of us tend to be lazy. We are like the fellow who went into a college bookshop and asked for a book that would help him with his economics course.

"Over here," the clerk said, "I have a wonderful little *Outline of Economics*. It will do half of your work for you."

"That's just what I'm looking for," replied the student. "Let me have two of them right away."

No one ever learned to typewrite or drive a car (or perhaps do any complex thing) by just *reading* a book about it. A book can explain the rules and preferred techniques, but only practice and application will develop useful skill. Suppose, for example, you demonstrate for someone how to drive a car. Then you give him a booklet explaining the rules of the road. By this kind of study he can learn enough about driving a car to answer almost any question, and even talk at length on how the controls of a car work. *In a verbal way* he will know "all" about it. But until he has had actual experience and practice in driving—until he develops habit patterns that enable him to drive without consciously thinking of the mechanics—he will not be a safe driver. When he is actually driving, he should not be thinking to himself: "Now if I want to go faster, I push my right foot down on the accelerator," or, "When I want to stop, I must be sure to remember to push the brake pedal with my right foot, not too hard or I will slam my face in the wheel . . . and be sure it's the brake, not the gas, I am pressing. . . ." Unless he drives largely by automatic habits, he is going to be an awkward, insecure, dangerous driver.

The same thing applies to using the principles of thinking in our everyday lives. Just *knowing* about them (even though we can make 100 per cent on any written test or stand before an audience and teach others our *booklore*) is not going to do us any good on life's busy firing line until we have made them a part of our automatic thinking habits.

This book contains only tested and workable tools for improving our thinking ability, but, like any tools, they do not work by themselves. We must learn to use them skillfully before they will help us live more successful and happier lives.

If we do not root these thinking habits deeply into our nervous systems, we are just not going to be able to use them when we need them most. Our greatest need for straight thinking usually occurs when things are happening fast and we must act quickly. If we are driving a car and a child runs in front

"Learn to think straight? Why should I waste my time like that?"

of us, whether we kill that child depends upon how well we have learned proper driving habits. In most emergencies, *it is our automatic habits that pull us through*—not how much verbal knowledge we have filed away in the dead-storage compartment of our brains.

To Get Started

The first step in putting the knowledge in this book to work is to start thinking in terms of "verbal maps." Use that notion at every possible opportunity. Whether you use these words in conversation is optional. The important thing is to use the idea of VERBAL MAPS *in your own thinking.* Instead of saying to yourself, "I've got to get this matter straight," for the next few months say instead, "I need a verbal map that adequately represents the territory." Instead of thinking, "That won't work," say to yourself, "That verbal map has no predictability."

As you study the principles in the coming chapters, you will find yourself saying, "Why, that's just common-sense thinking. I already know that." And **up to a point** you will be right.

All of us "know" the principles in this book and all of us use them now and then. But we have not understood them well enough *to apply them consistently.* And, as with all imperfectly learned skills, they leave us just when we most need them.

Here is a list of suggestions which people have found helpful in getting the most out of this book.

1. Remember that most of your future mistakes will be due to failure to apply the principles explained here. When something goes wrong, turn to the six **tools for thinking** explained

in the next six chapters, and see how they will help you to avoid similar mistakes.

2. One of the best ways to understand something is to try to explain it to others. If you want to test your own understanding of this new way of thinking, try springing it on some of your friends. Undoubtedly, you will discover something all teachers know—that the person giving instruction often learns more than the person receiving it. But always remember that the value of this book lies not in how well you can talk about it, but rather in the changes for the better it makes in your own thinking habits as shown in your day-by-day actions and problem solving.

3. Begin as soon as possible to apply the **tools for thinking** in the so-called little things of life. For training purposes, go out of your way to get the "feel" of them at work. Take time out to think before you act. Do everything you can to make the six **tools for thinking** a part of your permanent mental furniture.

4. After you read each section, stop and try to give examples of the principles from your own experience. After all, you are just wasting your time reading unless you can, somehow, begin to connect these principles with your own life. As Burke put it, "To read without reflecting is like eating without digesting."

5. Read each chapter at least twice. Remember, you are not merely reading for information; you are trying to form better thinking habits that help you get what you want out of life. You will find deeper meanings with each reading. Edison said, "Genius is 1 per cent inspiration and 99 per cent perspiration." Since you have read this far on *How to Develop Your Thinking*

Ability, you have the 1 per cent inspiration. Now, do a little sweating. You will find the results worth it.

To Sum Up

You will be wasting your time if you don't do your best to work these thinking habits deeply into your nervous system. In a sense, no one can teach you how to think or how to improve your thinking ability. It is only possible to explain more effective habits of thinking. Then it's your move.

Part II

THE SIX TOOLS FOR THINKING

are:

1. **So Far As I Know**
2. **Up to a Point**
3. **To Me**
4. **The What Index**
5. **The When Index**
6. **The Where Index**

In the next six chapters you will find a set of six tools that will enable you to increase your skill in making reliable verbal maps. These tools are words or phrases that you can add to your verbal maps. You will find that these phrases will act almost magically in helping you mature your thinking habits.

To make it easier for you to get acquainted with the **tools for thinking,** they will appear in boldface type throughout this book. Once you learn to use these tools, you will be amazed at how such simple and familiar phrases can do so much to increase your thinking ability.

Tool No. 1: SO FAR AS I KNOW

4

Only a God Knows All

An attitude of this kind—"You can't tell me anything about that"—has an effect quite similar to that of a pus sac in the brain.*

WENDELL JOHNSON

Mrs. Gladstone was downstairs entertaining guests who had just arrived for a dinner party. The conversation turned to the Bible, and there was a lively argument on the meaning of a certain passage. Soon one of the guests, hoping to end the discussion, remarked devoutly:

"There is One above Who knows all."

The cloud vanished from Mrs. Gladstone's face as she smiled sunnily and said:

"Yes, and William will be down in a few minutes."

In spite of Mrs. Gladstone's testimony to the contrary, **so far as I know,** no human being knows ALL about anything. Can you think of anything about which your knowledge is com-

* From *People in Quandaries* by Wendell Johnson. New York: Harper & Brothers. Copyright, 1946. Reprinted by permission.

plete? Large or small, old or new. Can you answer every question about an automobile or a grain of sand, a pencil or an inch of sewing thread, a BB shot or a human being?

Suppose you wanted to devote your lifetime to the study of a single lead pencil. Could you learn ALL about it? You might pick out a nice yellow one with a rubber eraser. You could then sit down and try to describe it as thoroughly as possible, giving the exact measurements and telling all you could about its construction and its uses. But to know EVERYTHING about the pencil, you would have to learn about the wood and the individual tree from which it was made. You would need to know the details of how the rubber was made. And you must not forget the metal in the little band holding the rubber. Then you would need to learn EVERYTHING about the lead, the glue, the paint, and the gold letters stamped on it.

You would then be well along in your attempt to learn ALL about the pencil. After a few years of study on the outside, you might begin to take the pencil apart and examine the inside details of that individual pencil. You would need to section it and make thousands of microscope slides to become acquainted with each fiber of wood and grain of graphite. And after you had exhausted your microscopic examination, you would then be ready to study the pencil from a molecular and atomic point of view.

Each molecule collides with other molecules many millions or billions of times per second, depending on the kind of molecule and the temperature. According to Sir Oliver Lodge, 250,000,000 atoms in a row only measure an inch and 100,000 electrons in a row equal the diameter of an atom. If you could count them at the rate of three per second twenty-four hours a day, it would take thousands of years just to count the atomic particles in your pencil. **So far as I know,** you could spend many lifetimes studying a single pencil from an atomic point of view and still not know ALL about it.

Fortunately we human beings manage to get along in this world without having complete verbal maps. No mechanic knows ALL about an automobile, but a good mechanic knows enough about it to keep it running fairly well. No doctor knows ALL about the human body, but they have become efficient in handling many of our ills. No person knows ALL about the art of cooking, but there are a lot of cooks who are good enough for my money.

"But," you may be saying to yourself, "ever since I got out of grammar school I've known that no one knew ALL about anything." The trouble is we *know* that, but frequently we do not *act* as though we knew it. As the old saying goes, "Everyone knows it, but the idea has not occurred to everyone."

The Key to Open-mindedness

When we really understand the significance of the fact that we don't know ALL about anything, it is easy to acquire habits of open-mindedness.

For instance, if you did know ALL about something, there would be no sense in keeping an open mind. There would be no need to listen to what anyone else had to tell you or to keep your eyes open in surveying the territory. Nothing would be new to you. Everything you planned would work out perfectly because your maps would be complete and have complete predictability! You would be justified in refusing to listen to what

"Nonsense! There couldn't be any whales in this bay."

others had to say, and you could forever renounce surveying the territory for new or different ideas.

We have all heard speeches on the desirability and the necessity of keeping open minds—but we are seldom told how to do it. The way to get and keep an open mind is to repeat to yourself: "I can't know ALL about ANYTHING. No one else knows ALL about ANYTHING. Therefore, I have no right to close my mind. I must watch for important facts that may have been overlooked. Some hidden factors may be found that will help me make my maps more adequate."

Edison said, "We don't know one-millionth of one per cent about anything." The people who make the most adequate verbal maps are those who are thoroughly aware of the incompleteness of their knowledge. As Cicero put it, "I am not ashamed to confess that I am ignorant of what I do not know."

Sometimes you hear people giving this advice: "Never act until you have ALL the facts." However wise that kind of advice may sound, it is impractical. Since we never have ALL the facts, we must decide when we have enough facts to make *adequate* verbal maps, and then act on them. "Life," said Samuel Butler, "is the art of drawing sufficient conclusions from insufficient premises."

The Tools for Thinking

Basically, this is a handbook for straight thinking.

The business of a handbook is to tell you how to translate knowledge into action. You will find in this chapter (and each of the next five chapters) a phrase you can use in your everyday thinking that will *automatically* start you using the principles for straight thinking presented here.

These phrases are called the **tools for thinking.**

The little phrase that is going to remind us that our maps are not complete and that we should keep an open mind is **"So far as I know."** For example, instead of saying, "She thinks only of herself," say, **"So far as I know,** she thinks only of herself."

Do not be misled by the simplicity of these tools. Everyone uses them occasionally—but few understand clearly the principles behind them. Because they are so obvious and well known, do not make the mistake of concluding this is child's stuff that you already apply. Hard as it may be to believe, you will still be developing insight into the use of these tools for months and years to come. They will bring to you unbelievable new discoveries, knowledge, and experiences. Don't take my word for it. Try it and see.

Six Blind Men and the Elephant

"Absolute certainty," said C. J. Keyser, "is a privilege of uneducated minds—and fanatics. It is, for scientific folks, an unattainable ideal."

The formula **so far as I know** will remind us that we may know only one side of the story. Because of our limited observations, we may be like the six blind men who examined the elephant.

The first blind man touched a leg and said, "An elephant is like a tree."

The second caught hold of his tail and said, "Why, an elephant is just like a rope."

The third touched his trunk. "Nonsense," he said, "an elephant is like a snake."

NO ONE SEES THINGS FROM ALL POINTS OF VIEW

The Six Blind Men

The fourth one touched his ear: "Why no, an elephant is like a leaf."

Number five pushed his hand against the side of the elephant: "I think an elephant is like a wall."

The sixth one came against the elephant's tusk: "You're all wrong," he said. "An elephant is like a spear."

Now these men were surveying the territory when they made their verbal maps. However, they did not survey *enough* of the territory to get an adequate picture. It is impossible for us to survey ALL the territory, and *we can never be absolutely sure we have surveyed enough to give us an adequate picture.* For no one can see things from ALL points of view.

Plutarch tells of a Roman divorced from his wife who was blamed by friends for the separation. "Was she not beautiful?" they asked. "Was she not chaste?"

The Roman held out his shoe for them to see and asked if it were not good-looking and well made. "Yet," he added, "none of you can tell where it pinches me."

A Single New Fact

Sometimes it takes only one new fact to upset our verbal maps. A museum in a certain eastern city was proud of its unusual attendance record. Obviously, the people in their fine city were well above average in their appreciation of the finer things in life. Recently, a little stone building was erected next door to the museum. During the next year, the attendance of the museum mysteriously fell off by over 100,000 visitors. What was the little stone building? It happened to be a comfort station!

We shall forever need the formula **so far as I know** to remind us that one additional fact may turn up to knock the stuffing out of our present maps!

I am not suggesting that you repeat the phrase **so far as I know** every time you open your mouth. People would think you were acting strangely. What I am advocating is that you *feel inside of you* that the verbal maps you make are not complete and that important considerations could be missing. In other words, whenever you start spouting words of wisdom, whenever you say what you think is so, you should silently add **so far as I know** for your own benefit.

SEE NEXT PAGE

When this attitude becomes deeply ingrained in your thinking, you will automatically be willing to hear what other people have to say. You will want to examine the facts that support their position. You will remember that no matter how much you know about something (even though you are a world authority on it!), there may still be facts that will enable you to mature your present ideas.

We Tend to Believe What We First Hear

Let us suppose Mr. Jones and Mr. Smith have an auto accident. Now we know from experience that if we happen to hear about the accident first from Mr. Smith, he will convince us that it was all Jones's fault and that Jones ought to be put in jail. However, if we happen to talk to Mr. Jones first, he will explain to us (in a thoroughly convincing manner) just how Mr. Smith was to blame. On the basis of the facts we get from him, we will deplore the fact that such dangerous drivers as

ONE OVERLOOKED FACT CAN MAKE A BIG DIFFERENCE

Mr. Smith are allowed on the road. When we realize that any one side (when it gets first shot) can usually present its own point of view in such a way as to convince us, we will understand the importance of learning to suspend our judgment by qualifying our verbal maps with **so far as I know.** We must not lend our ears and minds to only one side. We should try to understand both sides or three sides or a dozen sides, if a problem is that complex.

The Bible instructs us: "Prove all things; hold fast that which is good" (I Thess. 5:21). But once we have adopted a certain point of view, it is difficult for us to be open-minded toward another way of thinking or acting. "For what a man had rather were true," said Francis Bacon, "he more readily believes."

Little babies cannot fight as well as grownups. A new, baby idea coming into our head cannot compete with the old grown-up ones we have been embracing all our lives. We have to let the new ideas come in, grow, and mature. Frequently it is necessary to try to understand new ideas for days, weeks, or even years. When we feel we have done our best to understand a new point of view, we should then unleash our old ideas and have a real battle royal. The new ideas will have grown up and matured, and they will need no protection then.

In order to understand ideas that are different from the ones we now have, we must develop a perspective on them. If we argue with each little point when we first hear it, we will not be able to see the whole picture. If an army marched through a narrow gate, man by man, it would be easy to defeat. The same thing applies to understanding a new point of view. If

WE SHOULD HEAR BOTH SIDES BEFORE MAKING UP OUR MINDS

"I — er — uh — want to apologize for the way my boy. . . ."

we knock off the details, one by one, we are not giving them a chance *as a whole*. We must let them come out, line up, acquire their greatest strength, and then we must oppose them with whatever strength there is in our present point of view. And the ideas that remain after the clash of opinions has taken place are the ones we want. They are the "truths" that have emerged victorious.

"It is good to rub and polish our minds against those of others," said Montaigne. The tool **so far as I know** helps us to open our minds so that we can have a real clash of opinions and not just an unequal, unfair farce.

Take Pride in Open-mindedness

A closed mind is not a mind—it is a machine. It automatically spouts what is already in it. An open mind wants the truth that comes from the clash of opinions; a closed mind is only interested in continuing to believe whatever it now believes.

According to John Dewey, open-mindedness "may be defined as freedom from prejudice, partisanship, and such other habits as close the mind and make it unwilling to consider new problems and entertain new ideas. But it is something more active and positive than these words suggest. It is very different from empty-mindedness. While it *is* hospitality to new themes, facts, ideas, questions, it is not the kind of hospitality that would be indicated by hanging out a sign: 'Come right in; there is nobody at home.' It includes an active desire to listen to more sides than one; to give heed to facts from whatever source they come; to give full attention to alternative possibilities; to recognize the possibility of error even in the beliefs that are dearest to us." *

"The only people who make no mistakes," said H. L. Wayland, "are dead people. I saw a man last week who has not made a mistake for four thousand years. He was a mummy in the Egyptian department of the British Museum."

We should try to make people feel that they are invited to point out facts that will help us mature our verbal maps. We should make it clear that we do not regard a criticism or suggestion as a slap at our ego. We don't claim to know ALL about ANYTHING anyhow. "A man," said Pope, "should never be ashamed to own he has been in the wrong, which is but saying in other words that he is wiser today than he was yesterday."

To Sum Up

Since our maps are not complete, we have no right to close our minds on any subject. We must silently add **so far as I know** to everything we say because we never know when new facts will turn up that will enable us to mature our verbal maps. We must remember that "absolute certainty is a privilege of uneducated minds—and fanatics. It is, for scientific folks, an unattainable ideal."

* From *How We Think* by John Dewey. Reprinted by special permission of D. C. Heath and Company, Boston, Mass.

Tool No. 2: UP TO A POINT

5

Think in Terms of Degrees

All the great villains and small villains whom I met so frequently . . . were consistent men—unimaginative men who consistently believed in war as a means of settling disputes between nations; equally misguided men who consistently believed that war must be avoided at all hazards, no matter what the provocation; narrow men who consistently upheld the beliefs and acts of one political party and saw no good in any other; shortsighted men who consistently refused to see that the welfare of their own nation was dependent upon the welfare of every other nation; ignorant men who consistently thought that the policies of their own government should be supported and followed, whether those policies were right or wrong; dangerous men who consistently thought that all people with black skins are inferior to those with white skins; intolerant men who consistently believed that all people with white skins should be forced to accept all people with black skins as equals. And I know that any nation that cannot or will not avoid the dreadful pitfalls of consistency will be one with the dead empires. . . .

KENNETH ROBERTS*

* From *Lydia Bailey* by Kenneth Roberts. New York: Doubleday & Company, Inc. Copyright, 1947, by Kenneth Roberts and Anna M. Roberts. Reprinted by permission.

We live in a complicated world that requires careful mapping. We can *talk* about good things and bad things, black things and white things, true things and false things, beautiful things and ugly things, efficient and inefficient things. But where can we *find* things that are in every way as we have described them?

It is, for example, easy to label people or things as "good" and "bad." But most of the time a little bad comes packaged in with the good, and a little good with the bad. In other words, things are not usually completely good or completely bad. Few things, however good, are without some disadvantages. And almost nothing, however bad, is without a trace of good.

Scientists tell us that nothing in this world is pure black or pure white. If something were pure black it would absorb all the light that falls on it. All things, even lampblack, are known to reflect a small amount of light. If something were pure white, it would reflect 100 per cent of the light falling on it. No object has been found that reflects all the light that strikes it.

It is convenient to refer to things as being either poisonous or nonpoisonous. However, there is nothing so poisonous but that a small amount can be taken without harm. And there is nothing so nonpoisonous that a huge amount can be imbibed safely. Some of the most gruesome skulls and crossbones appear on iodine bottles, but a small amount of this "poisonous" iodine will not hurt anybody. For certain mouth conditions some dentists prescribe painting the gums with iodine. Water is regarded as "nonpoisonous," but the foremen of the torture chambers in the Middle Ages found that five quarts of water poured into the stomach of a human being made an excellent poison for their purposes—reliable in action, very painful, and not too fast or too slow. Anything can be poisonous if you absorb enough; nothing is poisonous if you take a sufficiently small quantity.

"It's Gotta Be This or That"

All of us have picked up EITHER-OR and ALL-or-NONE habits of thinking. We like to think of things as completely this way or completely that way. We seem to rebel against middle positions.

The Saturday Evening Post ran an article, "Can We Reform Our Bureaucrats?" that tried to present adequate verbal maps describing the way government offices are run. Many readers had trouble understanding the article. One person wrote to the editor:

> Whose side are you on? You knock the bureaucrats; then you say they are swell. You say bureaus are over-staffed. You say bureaus are under-staffed. . . .

The answer of the editor was to the point:

> It would be easier to paint the picture all black or all white. But big issues are seldom that simple; we prefer balanced, well-rounded reports.*

People with EITHER-OR habits of thinking tend to insist that verbal maps be drawn such that either ALL government

* Reprinted by permission of Curtis Publishing Company. Copyright, 1947.

THERE ARE MANY STEPS BETWEEN THE EXTREMES

officials be regarded as efficient or NO government officials be regarded as efficient. But unfortunately we live in a world that is generally too complex to be adequately covered by an EITHER-OR or an ALL-or-NONE verbal map. We live in a world where different individuals and organizations can show an infinite number of variations between efficiency and inefficiency.

Two Kinds of People

Someone with a twinkle in his eye once said, "There are two kinds of people in the world: those who always divide the people of the world into two kinds, and those who don't."

We live in a world of great diversity. For example, people do not come in two varieties: either good-looking or ugly. If we lined up a large group of people and arranged them according to degrees of homeliness and comeliness, we would have at one end of the line those who were alleged to "break a mirror at one glance." Next to them would be found those who were regarded as "just plain ugly." Then the ones we would call "unattractive." Then "so-so," then pretty, then "wow!"

We can't just fold humanity down the middle like a sheet of paper and have all the handsome ones on one side and those we call "ugly" on the other. Even those we call "ugly" may not be completely lacking in points of beauty, and vice versa. Katisha, a designing old maid in Gilbert and Sullivan's *Mikado,* realized that her face was not attractive. But she points out that people come from miles around to view her beautiful left shoulder blade—and (according to her) she has a right elbow with "a fascination that few can resist."

Actor Wallace Beery in commenting upon the way parts in the movies are often made too EITHER-ORish said:

> Most screen characters are either very good or very bad, a fact that often disturbs an actor as much as it does an intelligent observer. For no man is completely made from one piece of cloth, all good or all bad, all cruel or all tender. Instead, each person is a mixture of many things. . . .*

A Sport or a Tightwad?

When in New York, Arthur Brisbane, a well-known news commentator who died a millionaire, would dine at places like Delmonico's, the Hoffman House, and Dinty Moore's, where he tipped lavishly. In other words, he was a sport and a spender at these places. But Stanley Walker, who knew Brisbane well, tells us that occasionally Brisbane would drop into an inexpensive restaurant for a quick meal and leave an infuriated waitress picking up a nickel tip. Now what was Arthur Brisbane? Was he a sport, or was he a tightwad?

No answer to this question is possible so long as we insist upon thinking in EITHER-OR terms. *The life facts do not fit the EITHER-OR pattern, and the verbal maps we use to represent those life facts must not fit it either.* In some situations, at some times and places, Brisbane could be called a "sport." At other times and places he could be called a "tightwad." **Up to a point** he can be called both a "sport" and a "tightwad."

* Reprinted by permission of Curtis Publishing Company. Copyright, 1948.

THE DIFFERENCE BETWEEN A GOOD IDEA AND A BAD IDEA IS OFTEN A MATTER OF DEGREE

"I realize it's hot, Miss Stintchcomb, and that a comfortable receptionist is an efficient receptionist, but aren't we carrying things a bit too far?"

Up to a Point

The tool that will help us make adequate maps in a world where most things are not pure black or pure white is the phrase **"up to a point."**

Frequently we torment ourselves with questions that cannot be answered in ALL-or-NONE terms. For instance, here are some questions that can be answered only by a degree analysis:

QUESTION:	ANSWER:
Am I a success?	**Up to a point.**
Am I a failure?	**Up to a point.**
Am I superior to other people?	**Up to a point.**
Am I inferior to other people?	**Up to a point.**
Is Mary good-looking?	**Up to a point.**
Are politicians honest?	**Up to a point.**
Will Blotto shampoo remove dandruff?	**Up to a point.**
Will the rules for thinking in this book help me solve my problems?	**Up to a point.**

There are several phrases we frequently use when we think in terms of degrees. We can say, "*To some extent,* my car runs better when I change spark plugs," or, "The weather has affected my petunias *to quite a degree.*" Whatever phrase we use in our verbal maps, the important thing is to put a mental red flag on EITHER-OR and ALL-or-NONE statements. That red flag means: Possibly dangerous—survey the territory carefully.

Begin spotting every EITHER-OR statement you hear or find yourself making. Consider the problem from many points of view. You will gain remarkable insight into your life situations when you overcome an EITHER-OR attitude that may be now blocking your thought.

Either a Man or a Woman

But you may ask, "Aren't there some things that are adequately represented by an EITHER-OR verbal map? For instance, aren't people either men or women? Isn't this an EITHER-OR, ALL-or-NONE matter?"

Scientists who have made careful studies along this line tell us that it is even useful to think in terms of degrees here. A few things in this world are adequately mapped by EITHER-OR maps, but this is not one of them. A 100 per cent he-man and 100 per cent woman do not exist. Women have glands that produce male hormones and men have glands that produce female hormones. And on the average, women excrete 70 per cent as many male hormones as men. And men excrete on the average 40 per cent as many female hormones as women. As Roger J. Williams pointed out: "Any man who boasts that he is a 100 per cent he-man must, in order to substantiate his claim, bare a chest which is adorned with no telltale features and submit a sample of urine which contains no female sex hormones." *

Once a forty-four-year-old man with a normal sex life (he was married and had two sons) developed a tumor in his adrenal glands. The change in his glands caused by the tumor gradually made him more and more feminine. His breasts underwent development and his sex organs decreased in size.

* From *The Human Frontier* by Roger J. Williams. New York: Harcourt, Brace and Company, Inc. Copyright, 1946. Reprinted by permission.

A 100 PER CENT HE-MAN AND 100 PER CENT WOMAN DO NOT EXIST

"Watch him jump when I yell 'William.'"

His sex desire and potency disappeared, and he tended to lose his body hair. When the tumor was successfully removed by an operation, he lost the feminine characteristics and became a normal male again.

Most of the time nature manages to give us genital organs that are either male or female. But every now and then she really mixes things up. There are records of about fifty hermaphrodites—individuals with a complete set of both male and female organs!

So even such a thing as maleness and femaleness is not an EITHER-OR matter. Please note that I am not saying that EITHER-OR maps *never* represent life facts; but I am saying that in our daily life we tend to use the EITHER-OR pattern of thinking carelessly, and that many times we assume that things are EITHER-OR when careful thinking would reveal other possibilities.

The In-betweens

Most of the time, nature presents to us a continuous scale that shows no definite break between opposite ends. We do not have two kinds of weather: hot or cold. We do not even have three kinds of weather: hot, comfortable, and cold. During the period of a year, the temperature will range from uncomfortably hot to uncomfortably cold, and it does not skip a single degree. There may be more of some temperatures than others, but we will find all degrees between the extremes.

When people do not think in terms of degrees, they make verbal maps that violently distort the territory. Tom Brown says, "All politicians are crooked." A careful study will reveal that various politicians range from exceedingly honest to ex ceedingly dishonest. A verbal map like Tom's is quite inadequate because it represents only the lower part of the scale.

Dick Green is not so naïve as Tom. Dick says, "Politicians are either honest or dishonest." This verbal map represents the territory better, but it still misses the middle part of the scale. Harry Black has a three-valued approach. He says, "Politicians are either honest or dishonest or so-so."

This map represents the territory far more adequately than either of the other maps. It is rough, but for practical everyday purposes it may be satisfactory. However, it still does not represent the territory so adequately as possible. It implies that politicians come in three brands. Actually, there are as many degrees of honesty as there are politicians. If maps are to represent the territory as adequately as possible, they must reflect the varying degrees to be found in the territory.

Women's dresses come in all prices ranging from very cheap to very expensive. Most of the time, for practical purposes, it is satisfactory to classify dresses as low-cost, medium-cost, and high-cost. Even when it is practical to talk about the two ends and the middle of a scale, we should remember that the territory is not divided in this way but generally runs smoothly from one extreme to another.

For some of our purposes, we need verbal maps that are as precise as we can make them. At other times, we can get along with verbal maps that are only approximate. You alone must be the judge of how important it is that your verbal maps be precise. Different situations need different degrees of precision. For example, pajama manufacturers make three sizes: small, medium, and large; and the men get along all right. Pajamas

BEWARE OF THE POINT AT WHICH A LITTLE MORE MAY MAKE MORE THAN A LITTLE DIFFERENCE

"I believe in having fun, Graham, but only ***up to a point***!"

don't have to fit so well as shirts. Shirts have to be made in over a dozen different neck sizes and sleeve lengths in order to fit the range of men, who vary from small to large.

Up To What Point?

In order to find out **up to what point** the territory is hot or cold, black or white, good or bad, etc., it is necessary for us to observe carefully. Usually it is not very helpful for us to know that Henry Jones is honest **up to a point.** We need to know **up to what point.** What kind of reputation does he have? Is he known to take everything that isn't nailed down? Is he no more honest than the system demands? Can he be trusted in small things? Can he be trusted in large things? Does it seem likely that you can place any amount of confidence and trust in Henry's honesty?

As with the other tools for thinking, when we use **up to a point** *we must consider the facts.* In trying to find out **up to what point** Henry Jones is honest, we would assemble all the data and information we can. We make a **so far as I know now** decision, and, if we are smart, we will keep our minds open for further evidence that will either confirm or reverse the decision. Henry Jones is a process and the point he's up to can change from time to time.

If the Territory Is Not Consistent

Have you noticed that when we begin to argue with certain people, they will insist we either agree with them 100 per cent or disagree with them 100 per cent? It annoys them for us to agree partly or disagree partly. They want to maintain that he who is not with them 100 per cent is against them—ALL or NONE.

We must have patience with those who would push us toward an extreme position. If we fall into their trap, we will be making verbal maps that do not adequately represent the territory, and they will have no trouble making us appear foolish. We must stand our own ground and not be intimidated. We must explain that it is not our fault that things are not all black or all white; we must make our maps represent the territory as WE see it. Remember: the narrower the mind, the broader the statement.

Most of the time, maps are more adequate if they say:

"Many" or "most" instead of ALL.
"Usually" instead of ALWAYS.
"Seldom" instead of NEVER.
"Similar" instead of SAME.

When someone insists that it has "gotta be this or that," ask him how he knows. Unfortunately, truth does not usually do a very thorough job of organizing herself along EITHER-OR lines. If we are going to *follow* truth wherever she may lead, we have to get over our habits of *guiding* her into an EITHER-OR corral.

Beware of Selected Examples

It is easy to select convincing examples implying that ALL government bureaus are inefficient, ALL businessmen are greedy, woman is fickle, man is evil, the stars control our destinies, or the end justifies the means. An example proves only that SOME of the things in question work that way. The prob-

HOW MANY MAKES A DIFFERENCE

lem before the careful thinker is: **Up to what point** does the entire group act that way?

It is only by making a count of *unselected examples* that we can ever find **up to what point** a generalization adequately represents the territory. No amount of *selected* examples, however convincing, can be relied upon. Only by checking things as they run, that is, by random sampling, can we free ourselves from the persistent tendency to select things that prove our point and to ignore things on the other side.

The astrologers claim that people born under the sign of Libra should have musical talent. One person who tried to find out **up to what point** this map represents the territory, checked the birthdays of 1498 musicians. According to his figures, "fewer are born under Libra than under any sign except Scorpio."

Once you get used to looking for ways to rate the **up-to-a-pointness** of your verbal maps, you will be able to think of many clever ways to test them that have not occurred to you or perhaps to anyone else before. People who make accurate counts of random samples to find **up to what point** their verbal maps represent the territory add to the world's store of useful knowledge. Those who insist on "proving" their point by beautifully selected examples simply perpetuate their own varieties of misinformation and nonsense. The thousands of hours they spend during their lifetime thinking and reasoning about things will not leave them or anyone else any wiser. The people who keep quiet for a while and systematically check things are the ones who do their part to increase the amount of reliable knowledge in circulation.

The Last Straw

Life is a matter of making wise choices—of knowing when to draw the line. Professor Thorndike pointed out if you put a frog in a pan of cold water and then *gradually* raise the temperature degree by degree, you can cook him to death and he will not be aroused enough to jump out of the pan. In like manner, people who are not vigilant can be deprived of their liberty (or anything else they value) without knowing what is going on. We must not be deceived by the degree nature of things. There's a certain point at which a large number of small changes add up to an important difference without any break or jump.

The hair on a man's chin doesn't jump out all of a sudden. It grows slowly and quietly, and there is no definite point at which the complexion suddenly changes from a skin you like to touch to a rough beard. But that doesn't keep us from drawing the razor when we realize that our beard has grown beyond the point we think proper.

In preparing adequate verbal maps, then, we must bear in mind that there is usually no sharp line that divides opposites. NO ONE IS 100%:

Sane or insane
Intelligent or unintelligent
Good or bad
Black or white
Efficient or inefficient
Beautiful or ugly
Chic or sloppy
Musical or nonmusical
Fast or slow
Quick-tempered or calm

THERE IS A POINT AT WHICH ONE MORE WILL MAKE MORE DIFFERENCE THAN ALL BEFORE

"Now don't you worry about me, pal. Know just when to stop."

"Don't worry about me. Know JUST WHEN to stop."

But just because there is no sharp line between a heavy load and a light load, we must not assume there's no difference. We must not be like the man who loaded his camel one straw at a time hoping the additional weight of a single straw would never break its back.

If we are to make maps that ADEQUATELY represent the territory, we must:

1. Look for the degree nature of things.
2. Hunt for the point at which a little more *may make more than a little difference.* We must be aware that there is a point at which a single extra straw may make more difference than the thousands of straws that have gone before.

Only people who are in the habit of thinking in terms of degrees and who try to find **up to what point** a map fits the territory, will be really at home in this world. For others, there will be more things to raise their blood pressure than are really necessary. Expecting to find ALL-or-NONE, they have a tough time reconciling themselves to a degree-world, stocked mainly with *more or less.*

To Sum Up

We live in a subtle world in which things usually are not pure black or pure white. If our maps are to represent things adequately, we cannot make them either completely black or completely white. The tool **up to a point** will remind us that things vary from NONE TO ALL, and that we must *stop, look,* and *listen* to become familiar enough with the territory to make an adequate verbal map that has predictability.

Tool No. 3: TO ME

6

Look Who's Talking

If I look up and you look down
Upon the biggest man in town,
You'll see his head and ears and nose,
I'll see his feet and knees and toes.
And though it is one man we see,
You'll swear he's A, I'll swear he's B.

GEORGE H. PRESTON *

Companies in the soap business have made millions of dollars by convincing the public that a person is no judge of whether or not he smells. They have thoroughly put across the message that other people can sniff things that aren't apparent to us no matter how hard we try. The B.O. (Body Odor) advertising has told us that we don't know all about ourselves, and that sometimes even our best friends won't tell us.

Now it seems **to me** that avoiding M.O. (Mental One-

* From *Psychiatry for the Curious* by George H. Preston. New York: Farrar & Rinehart, Inc. Copyright, 1940, by George H. Preston. Reprinted by permission.

sidedness) is just as important as avoiding B.O. Avoiding M.O. requires, unfortunately, a little more than the application of soap. When we have M.O., sometimes even our best friends *can't* tell us—*they may have the same kind of M.O. we have.* In this chapter we will find a **tool for thinking** that will remind us that we smell mentally just as much as the soap ads say we do physically.

But first, let us find out:

How We Get M.O. (Mental One-sidedness)

Each of us lives a life that never has been, or never will be, exactly like that of any other human being. The children of this world are brought up in homes which range from squalid one-room shacks about to fall apart to large palaces with dozens of servants. According to the preferences of their parents, they may be trained in one of several dozen religions and many political philosophies. They may be reared on a farm or in a small town; they may grow up in the mountains à la Dogpatch, or they may live in a large metropolitan city where milk comes from a bottle. There are some who have had no schooling and cannot read or write, and there are others who spend as much as a quarter of a century in formal education. Each county in every state has a particular set of passions and prejudices that are more or less different from those of its neighbors. Little children lap up the prevalent prejudices and local feelings as readily as they lap up their food.

Differing Backgrounds

If a blind man bumped into you on the street, you wouldn't be likely to get mad at him. You would realize that due to the

"My fourth. You?"

way he was born or to something that happened to him after he was born, he is just unable to see the things you can see.

But when people disagree with us on personal, social, business, and political matters, we may get mad at them because we feel they are either mean or stupid. We forget that we believe what we happen to believe because of our glands, the people we've been with, the books we've read, and the experiences we've had.

Things that seem natural to one group of people may be shocking to another. For example, in 1924 a Japanese museum held an exhibition of some European paintings and statues. Rodin's sculpture "The Kiss" was considered too indecent for public view. A bamboo screen had to be placed around it. Since the United States occupation, the Japanese seem to be, at least in one particular, adopting Western ways. Kisses are now permitted in Japanese motions pictures.

Even as European a country as Finland has been slow in accepting the kiss. In 1915, it was regarded as improper, although the same Finns had no objection to mixed bathing *au naturel.* An estimated one-third of the people in the world don't kiss at all. Not only the Japanese, but the Chinese, Malayans, Polynesians, Eskimos, and practically all the aboriginal tribes find kissing uninteresting or immoral. Some think it's more fun to blow into each other's ears; some Eskimos find rubbing noses more thrilling. A city in ancient Greece once passed a law that any man who kissed his wife in public should be put to death.*

* Taken from *This Week Magazine.* Copyright, 1949, by the United Newspapers Magazine Corporation.

WHAT WE LIKE DEPENDS ON WHAT WE'RE USED TO

"Your eyes . . . your lips . . . your hair. . . ."

What seems natural or common sense to us depends on when, where, and with whom we grew up. In view of our differing backgrounds, is it any wonder that we frequently disagree with each other?

Up to a Point, the World Is What We Make It

Phenyl-thio-carbimide (PTC) has been called the "tolerance chemical." According to Dr. Albert F. Blakeslee, one out of five people find it tasteless. About 65 per cent find it bitter. Five per cent call it sour, 2 per cent insist that it is sweet, and 5 per cent are sure it is salty. Other people who have tasted it report such sensations as bitter almonds, camphor, and sulfur.

Would you like to test yourself and your friends with paper that has been dipped in PTC? If you will send 10 cents to the American Genetic Association, 1507 M Street, N.W., Washington 5, D.C., you will receive enough PTC paper to test fifty people. You simply put a small piece of this harmless paper in your mouth and chew it for a few seconds to know how it tastes **to you.**

After you test yourself and your friends and get into some arguments over whether the paper is or is not tasteless, bitter, sour, salty, etc., you should reread this chapter. Don't try arguing what the taste *really* is. There is no one answer on which all sensible people can agree. This simple, fascinating experiment will do more to impress on you the principles in this chapter than two hours of straight reading. Try it and see.

To Some Extent, We Create Our Facts

"We see things not as they are," said the wise man, "but as we are." Most of us have not learned to be aware of the part our nervous system plays in reporting facts. When we say, "This stew is good," or, "This flower is red," or, "The PTC paper tastes bitter," we think we are talking about qualities that are completely in the stew, flower, or paper.

But, for example, the flower itself isn't red. The red is created by our apparatus for seeing and interpreting. A flower reflects light waves of a certain wavelength. These light waves are picked up by the lenses of the eyes and focused on the retina of each eye. They are then changed into electrical impulses which travel along the two million fibers that make up the optic nerves leading from the eyes to the brain. In the visual cortex of the brain the incoming electrochemical impulses are *made into the sensation we call "red."* But light waves are not red or any other color. They are electromagnetic energies similar to heat rays, cosmic rays, and X rays. We create the "red" in our own nervous systems. In other words, the red we see is *a joint product of what is outside of us and our own machinery for observing.* Many people have nervous systems that do not change wavelengths of 6500 Ångström units (an Ångström unit is 1/100,000,000 of a centimeter) into red. What others see as red, they will see as a different color, or perhaps in tones of gray.

We see reality through a mirror that partially transmits and partially reflects. We see things that are outside of us, but we see them bathed in "reflections" from our own minds.

Add "To Me" to Your Verbal Maps

If you say, "Pistachio ice cream is good," remember that you are talking about your own nervous system, or your own reaction to pistachio ice cream. If the man next to you says, "Pis-

..chio ice cream is terrible," remember that he is talking about himself just as much as he is talking about pistachio ice cream. It is stupid to get into an argument about whether pistachio ice cream is, or is not, delectable. *Such arguments cannot lead to agreement simply because they are not arguments about what is outside of people.* Each person is simply reporting the way his own nervous system works—BUT HIS LANGUAGE MISLEADINGLY IMPLIES THAT HE IS TALKING ONLY ABOUT ICE CREAM.

If you add **to me** to your verbal maps, you will side-step foolish disagreements of this sort. If you say, "**To me** pistachio ice cream is good," you have made a map that fits *your territory.* If the person next to you says, "**To me** pistachio ice cream tastes terrible," he has made a map that fits *his territory* and neither map will be regarded as conflicting with the other.

There are many phrases that can remind us of the part we play in the production of knowledge. In this book we are using the phrase **to me** (and variations like **to you, to him, to her,** and **to them**). Other phrases such as, "From my point of view," "As I see it," or, "Apparently," are often used for the same purpose: to remind us that a mortal human being is talking.

Your Reaction Depends on What You Are Used To

Suppose you have three buckets of water in front of you. One bucket has been cooled down to 40 degrees, the middle one is about 80 degrees, and the other one is quite warm at about 120 degrees. You put your right hand in the bucket of cold water and your left hand in the bucket of hot water. Let them get accustomed to it for a minute. Then if you put your

YOUR REACTION DEPENDS ON WHAT YOU ARE USED TO

right hand into the middle bucket, it will feel warm. And if you put your left hand in the middle bucket, it will feel cold. If you put both hands in the middle bucket at the same time, it will feel warm to your right hand and cold to your left.

In other words, even your left hand will not agree with your right if it has been subjected to different conditions. In this case you could not say, "**To me** the middle bucket is hot (or cold)." You would have to be even more specific: "**To my right hand** the middle bucket is warm, but **to my left hand** it is cold."

When we add **to me** to our verbal maps, we will be reminded that we should take our nervous systems into account. It helps us realize that when we give judgments we are talking about ourselves (and what we are used to) just as much as we are talking about the things outside us.

The Importance of a Point of View

"It's easy to spot a well-informed man," a wit once said, "his opinions are just like your own."

When the Alsatian pastor John Frederick Oberlin found two people disagreeing with each other, he would get them to sit down at opposite ends of a table in his study. He would then point to a picture on the wall and say, "John, what do you see in that picture?" John would look up and say, "I see a flower." Then he would say, "Bill, what do you see?" And Bill would say, "No, he's wrong. That's a bird." Then John and Bill would start arguing again. He would let them argue heatedly for a while and then ask them to exchange places at the table. When they changed their point of view, they found that the picture from one end of the table looked like a flower, and from the other end it looked like a bird. Then the kindly pastor would point out: "A lot depends upon your point of view."

We cannot get along in this world and keep our blood pressure down if we do not liberally sprinkle our verbal maps with **to me's.** No matter how carefully we map the territory, we can only say, "This is the way I see it. This is the way things are **to me.**"

We have no right to assume that our way of seeing things is the only proper way; we have no right to assume that all people who disagree with us are fools. We are different from other people by heredity, and we are different from them by training, too. Our point of view is different and our interests are different; hence, we can expect that people with other points of view will reach other conclusions based upon THEIR points of view, experiences, and data.

Someone said jokingly, "Tolerance is pretending that opinions which disagree with yours are not nonsense." The phrase **to me** is not designed to develop this superficial kind of tolerance. Nor should adding **to me** to our verbal maps always indicate that everyone is equally right and that one plan is just as good (that is, brings just as much happiness) as another. Instead, the phrase **to me** should help us understand why we often disagree with other people and why they disagree with us. This understanding will help us convert them to our point of view, or, on the other hand, it will help us accept their point of view, if theirs is more mature.

Our Personal Interests Blind Us

"It's interesting," wrote William J. Reilly, "to watch how our views change with our personal interests. On one occasion,

"Dad, can the insurance doctor keep your ulcers from coming back?"

when a boy, I went fishing with three other boys. On the way to the river we decided that the 'catch' should be pooled and divided equally among all of us. And I agreed wholeheartedly. I felt that it was absolutely fair and square. But during the course of the day, I found that I was leading the rest in the number of fish caught, and my attitude toward the whole proposition of dividing the catch began to change. By the time the day was over and there was no further chance of anyone else catching as many fish as I had, I became violently opposed to our original proposition, and told the boys that I couldn't understand why a good fisherman should be penalized because of the incompetence and bad luck of his associates." *

Whenever our personal interests are at stake, we need the tool **to me** to remind us that we may be seeing things through distorted glasses. Most of us have minds that do a pretty good job of "protecting" us from information we prefer not to hear. Grogan was dying, and he asked his wife and children to listen to his last instructions:

"There's Finnegan; he owes us ten dollars."

"'Tis a blessed thing," she said, "that you still have all your senses."

"And there's Dilligan; he owes us fifteen dollars."

"How wonderful," she said to the others, "to see the poor man speakin' so sensible-like!"

"And don't forget," said Grogan, "that we owe four dollars to the butcher."

"Oh," she said, "will ye listen to the man ravin'!"

* From *The Twelve Rules for Straight Thinking* by William J. Reilly. New York: Harper & Brothers. Copyright, 1935, 1938, 1947. Reprinted by permission.

Our minds tend to let in only what fits in with our personal feelings and interests. Charles Darwin was aware of this tendency and he always made it a point to write down any evidence that did not fit in with his scientific theories. He knew how easy it is to forget things that do not fit in with one's hopes and desires.

Rationalization

We protect ourselves from facing facts by cleverly twisting our thinking. This twisting is called "rationalization." When we rationalize we think up a reason to justify whatever we do or think.

A country parson was preaching fervently against all the common sins, ranging from murder to crap shooting. In her pew, a devout old woman rocked and swayed, intoning: "Amen—Amen. Praise God!" at each prohibition. Then the parson started on the subject of snuff dipping. The pious old lady sat bolt upright and muttered to herself, "Now he done stopped preachin' and took to meddlin'."

It seems we can see what people are talking about as long as they don't mean *us*. Rationalization changes preaching into meddling at the point we want. Rationalization enables us to hurt other people's feelings under the noble banner of "honest frankness." It also lets us get mad at the "unwarranted rudeness" of other people when they do the same thing. Rationalization enables us to spend extravagantly when we want to, under the high-sounding ideal of "keeping money in circulation." It also permits us to act like a tightwad when we so desire because, after all, "A penny saved is a penny earned." Rationalization lets us judge groups we do not like by their

ONE MAN'S MEAT MAY BE ANOTHER'S POISON

Ted Key

worst examples but allows us to feel outraged when someone "misjudges" our group by pointing to one not up to par. Rationalization enables us to stir up trouble among people because "a person has a right to know what is being said about him by people who pretend to be his friends." It also lets us condemn other people when they do the same thing because "there is no troublemaker like someone who gossips and spreads rumors." In short, when we rationalize, we can explain anything and everything in such a way that no matter what we do, WE are always right and THE OTHER FELLOW is always wrong—even when he does the same thing! "Every way of a man is right in his own eyes," the Bible warns us (Proverbs 21:2).

I have never found anyone (myself included) who was not excellent at rationalizing. If we could learn to think straight just half as well as we have learned to rationalize, we would get rid of about half of our problems and be twice as happy.

To Sum Up

Truth may order us to advance, but we seldom get far when our prejudices and habits are in the way. Robert Burns recognized our difficulty when he wrote:

> Oh wad some power the giftie gie us
> To see oursels as ithers see us!

The tool **to me** will remind us that our attitudes and opinions are determined by the genes we were born with and the way we were brought up. This tool warns us that our minds cleverly and subtly twist things to fit in with our personal interests. We are capable of rationalizing whatever we do or say

—as Benjamin Franklin put it: "So convenient a thing it is to be a *reasonable creature,* since it enables one to find or make a reason for everything one has a mind to do."

The tool to me may not always keep us from disagreeing with other people, but it may keep us from disagreeing in a disagreeable way.

Tool No. 4: THE WHAT INDEX

7

Differences May Make a Difference

Nature never rhymes her children nor makes two men alike.
RALPH WALDO EMERSON.

In the past three chapters we have reviewed our plight as thinkers who, by the nature of things, must struggle along with incomplete knowledge in a degree world with minds that have personal idiosyncrasies. And we have only begun to find out about things that threaten to upset our verbal maps if we are not vividly aware of them. In this and the following two chapters, we will discuss other characteristics of the world that make it difficult for us to produce adequate maps. As in the last three chapters, we will find **tools for thinking** that will keep these monkey wrenches from jamming our mental machinery for making reliable verbal maps.

We live in a world in which no two things are alike in ALL respects. We cannot, for example, meet one or two or even a dozen Russians and generalize about ALL Russians. We cannot use one electric razor and make verbal maps that cover ALL electric razors. Each individual is in some ways unique.

Up to a Point, They're All Different

Look anywhere you want for two things that are alike in all respects: two grains of sand, two peas in a pod, two people, two fingernails, two leaves on a tree, or two sticks of chewing gum. You will find many things that are similar. You will have no trouble finding things that *for your purposes* are interchangeable. But **so far as I know** you will never find two things that are absolutely identical.

In spite of mass production and careful inspection, no two cars ever produced at a factory are absolutely identical. They may look alike from outside the show window and the price on each may be the same, but each car will have its own particular pattern of strength and weakness. Various nuts and bolts and screws will be tightened to different degrees and will rattle apart at different times. Microscopic flaws and cracks in the metal parts will exist in different places and will play different parts in the processes of deterioration.

The packages of toothpicks and matches we buy are amazingly alike—**up to a point.** But when we pull out a magnifying glass (or, if necessary, a microscope) the differences begin to show up.

Distance makes for seeing similarities: nearness helps us to see differences. Two cars that are three miles away (even though different models and colors) will seem identical to the unaided eye. As we get closer, the differences are noticeable. From across a pasture, it would be difficult to tell a bull from a cow, but we make no mistake at close range. From down the block, two lampposts may look identical. From our yard, the leaves on the neighbor's trees look alike. From across the room,

DISTANCE MAKES THINGS APPEAR SIMILAR; NEARNESS HELPS US SEE DIFFERENCES

"Thank goodness, my Billy doesn't climb trees like that."

"Billy—!"

it is difficult to distinguish two phonograph records from the same album. If we hold two new razor blades from the same package in our hand, we may have difficulty distinguishing between them—until we use a magnifying glass to get us closer. Two highly polished steel balls may appear identical even with a powerful magnifying glass—but differences will be easily seen when a microscope brings us a thousand times closer.

How Group Words Mislead Us

As should be apparent by now, we live in a world where we can easily be misled by the words we use if we do not automatically remember that two things may be labeled alike and yet act quite differently. This is something that most of us "know," but few people ever think about the problem enough to realize its extensive implications and to figure out how they can meet it in their thinking habits. Instead, we blithely go on using language and thinking habits that often lead us to make fools of ourselves.

Please remember: Group words (such as *"man," "house," "dog," "Californian," "tree,"* etc.—that is, all collective and abstract nouns) do not tell WHAT KIND, WHEN, and WHERE. Due to faulty language and thinking habits all of us have picked up from our teachers, parents, playmates, and others, we tend to assume we are talking about *something definite and specific* when we use a group word, as, for instance, "dog."

Actually animals that are properly labeled "dog" will range from sassy little handfuls of caninity like the Mexican Chihuahua to massive great Danes. Dogs will range from sweet-

"Tell me something. Are ALL French sailors like you?"

tempered and patient animals that will take any amount of abuse from children whom they love to paranoiac and pugnacious mutts that probably dream of such delicious adventures as severing human jugular veins. Under the word "dog" you'll find sickly, persnickity animals that have grown accustomed to 50-cents-a-pound hamburger (that has been properly cooked and salted) to animals that do well for themselves just foraging off neighborhood garbage cans. Dogs may be found that are fit only for cuddling on milady's lap. There are other dogs that will protect the house against burglars, rescue drowning children, do tricks, such as jumping through flaming rings and barking to ten, herd sheep, go on sentry duty, or carry a cask of brandy to people lost in the snow. Anyone who says that he likes "dogs" is liking a whole lot—and anyone who says he doesn't like "dogs" is disliking a whole lot.

If our language is to reflect reality—if we are to make maps that represent the territory and have a high degree of predictability—we must remember that thinking in terms of groups can often mislead us if we are not aware of the dangers. There are no automobiles-in-general, dogs-in-general, or men-in-general adrift in our world. There are only specific individuals of many different kinds that do things in definite places at definite times, and *all these individuals may act in some ways different from others that are labeled by the same name.*

The What Index

The **tool for thinking** that helps us think in terms of individuals is called the **what index.** This is simply a number added to a group word. For example:

DON'T BE MISLED BY WORDS—
DOG_1 IS NOT DOG_2

"I love dogs. Man's best friend, you know."

"We'd better read that chapter on index numbers tonight."

Dog$_1$, dog$_2$, dog$_3$ .... etc.
Man$_1$, man$_2$, man$_3$ .... etc.
Chair$_1$, chair$_2$, chair$_3$ .... etc.

Please reread the following definition of the **what index** several times; then look at it again frequently while you are finishing this chapter:

The **what index** *is simply a number that is added to a group word to give us a feeling of referring to a specific person or thing.*

The basic principle of this entire chapter is that no two individuals are identical. Here is how we say it with **index numbers:**

Dog$_1$(*a bulldog*) IS NOT **dog$_2$**(*a great Dane*).
Dog$_2$(*a great Dane*) IS NOT **dog$_3$**(*a poodle*), etc., etc.

Also:

Dog$_1$(*a bulldog with a white ring around left eye*)

IS NOT

Dog$_2$(*a bulldog with ring around both eyes*)

IS NOT

Dog$_3$(*a bulldog with scar between eyes*) etc., etc.

When we apply the **index numbers** to people, we find that:

Man$_1$ IS NOT **man$_2$**.
Man$_2$ IS NOT **man$_3$**.
Man$_3$ IS NOT **man$_4$**.

. . . **Man$_{16}$** IS NOT **man$_{17}$**, . . . etc.

When we stop to think about it, we can see that we've been using **index numbers** all our lives—but in the past we've just used them for certain things. For example, we assign **index numbers** to our streets and houses, such as 142 S.W. 3d Street. We apply **index numbers** to the floors of buildings ($floor_1$, $floor_2$, $floor_3$, etc.). The armed services assign serial numbers to all personnel. So why not use distinguishing numbers with all group words to remind us of differences between individual people and things?

Mental Ghosts

When Peter was five years old, his mother ran away with a traveling salesman. After a year, his father married a woman who had two daughters several years older than Peter. The older girls made fun of Peter and giggled at him. He would try to "get even" by fighting back. The stepmother would then separate them and scold Peter for fighting. As he grew up, Peter felt more and more resentment toward these "women" in his life.

At the age of sixteen he got a job, left home, and lived by himself. At the grocery store where he was working he met a young girl, went out with her a few times, and fell deeply in love with her—until she jilted him in favor of a flashy young chap who had just acquired a shiny new convertible.

Just as he was beginning to decide that "women" were no good, he met a sympathetic young lady with a beautiful profile who made him forget his "troubles." They became engaged shortly before he went into the army. Before Peter went overseas, he got a short leave. On returning home for a surprise visit, he found his fiancée with another man in her bedroom.

COW$_1$ IS NOT COW$_2$
(SOMETIMES IT'S A LOT OF BULL)

"Don't bother me. I know my cows."

Peter was shocked and hurt. But he told himself he should have expected it. He should have known that "women" (ALL women) were no good. Beginning with his mother who had deserted him, with his stepmother and her two brats, with the first girl who had jilted him and the second one who was untrue, they were "all alike" : insincere, heartless, and not to be trusted at all. He made up his mind never to be fooled by "women" again. Now the "ghosts" of the women he has known are projected onto every girl he meets. "Girls," he advises, "are O.K. for a little adventure. But if you have any sense you won't take them seriously. They're all just alike. They'll fool you every time."

Peter needs these **index numbers** badly. He is confusing ALL women with the few with whom he has had unfortunate experiences. His unfortunate experiences with **$woman_1$**, **$woman_2$**, **$woman_3$**, **$woman_4$**, and **$woman_5$**, make him unable to see clearly **$woman_6$**, **$woman_7$**, **$woman_8$**, **$woman_9$**, etc. He needs the **index numbers** to help him get these "ghosts" out of his mind. He has a mental set that makes him see all women as similar —he has become so embittered that he is actually unable to admit the possibility of differences that make a difference.

Unindexed words are sometimes like mental ghosts. They recall to our minds the shapes of things in the past. If it were possible to know ALL about something and if the world did not keep changing, then we could be sure that our past experiences would be perfect guides for the future. We could summon up these ghosts of the past and let them tell us how to act for all time. But as long as we live in a changing world about which our knowledge is incomplete, we must be mighty careful how we rely upon the "lessons" we have absorbed in the past.

Similarities and Differences

The group word "women" reminds us of the similarities among all the things labeled by the word "women." The **index numbers** remind us of the differences that exist among all "women."

If we are to think maturely, we must be aware of *both* similarities and differences. We will get into trouble, for example, if we act as though ALL women are similar in ALL respects. We will also get into trouble if we act as though ALL women are different in ALL respects. By adding **index numbers** to our group words, we can achieve a way of thinking and speaking that will help remind us of both similarities and differences. By using the **index numbers** we can theoretically have a specific word or symbol for every person and thing in the universe!

Our habit of talking about THE American woman, THE typical Californian, or THE Southerner tends to make us overlook the great differences that exist between individuals that are so labeled as "types." Granted that individuals in the above-mentioned groups may be similar in one or more ways, the differences for *our* purposes may often be more important than the similarities. At any rate, we cannot make adequate verbal maps if we overemphasize either the differences or the similarities. We must be aware of both. *Our ordinary language tends to imply similarity simply because we label things by the same name.* We need the **index numbers** to remind us of differences.

SIMILARITIES CAN MISLEAD US

Give It Time to Sink In

When you first read this, you may feel that a mountain is being made out of a molehill and that all this discussion of similarities and differences about **dog_1, dog_2, dog_3**, etc., is not for you. But if you will continue to think about these principles, you will find that they have a *thoroughly practical* application in YOUR everyday life. It is not easy to understand the underlying significance of the **index numbers** by reading about them. You must live with them a while to find out what they can mean to you in your problem solving.

You may not understand the importance of **index numbers** until you've been chagrined several times because you did not notice differences between objects that were labeled alike but that for YOUR purposes acted differently. You must learn to say to yourself, "I know that **business $client_1$** is not **business $client_2$**, that **$politician_1$** is not **$politician_2$**," and so on.

You will have to notice for yourself how deeply set is your tendency to regard things labeled by the same name as the same. . . .

Now let us find out more about how the **index numbers** can help us:

Averages Do Not Tell Us Anything about Man_1 or $Thing_1$

Generalizations that correctly apply to groups may be misleading when slapped on any particular individual in the group. For example, suppose a man setting up a shoe store read that the average man wears an 8½B shoe. He would go out of business in a hurry if he ordered nothing but 8½B shoes.

Actually, this size is worn by only a small percentage of the people. A shoe store must fit **man$_1$, man$_2$, man$_3$**, etc. Frequently an average does not fit many individuals. No matter how accurate your average picture is, you still do not know whether it actually fits a particular individual (**man$_1$**, or **woman$_1$**, or **thing$_1$**) until you use your own eyes and survey the territory for yourself.

Often it is convenient to have average or general pictures of things. In planning a generator plant, an electric company will need reliable figures about the *average* amount of electricity used in the homes in its territory. In planning our budget, we will need to know the *average* amount we spend on food, clothing, and other items. We frequently get so used to thinking in terms of averages that we forget they are only useful in dealing with groups. An average figure, no matter how accurate, will not tell us anything definite about a given individual. *The only way we will get an adequate map of a specific individual is to survey the territory.*

Let me repeat: no matter how accurate an average picture is, we cannot be sure that it applies to any individual person or thing until we examine the territory. An average map is valid only so long as we are talking about a group. For example, suppose you knew that during the last year your average meal cost 78 cents. From this figure you could not predict that your lunch tomorrow will cost exactly 78 cents. It may be more or less.

Hunt for Differences That Make a Difference

I have tucked away in my brain a generalized notion of lions. According to my ideas, lions are pretty ferocious animals.

BOY$_1$ IS NOT BOY$_2$

"But you laughed when Henry Aldrich did it."

This generalization reminds me to stay away from uncaged lions. Now I am not going to use the **index numbers** in such a way as to get chewed up. I am not going overboard by saying, "**Lion**$_1$ is not **lion**$_2$, **lion**$_2$ is not **lion**$_3$, etc., and perhaps **lion**$_3$ being different from **lion**$_2$ will not attack me." Despite the fact that I know each of these lions is in some ways different, I am not going to let the **index numbers** lead me into surveying *that* particular territory for myself. I would regard that as a misuse of the **index numbers.**

Only *you* can decide when it is appropriate to use this tool. The principle is true in all situations: **lion**$_1$ is not **lion**$_2$. However, for MY purposes, **lion**$_1$ may act the same as **lion**$_2$. We know as a scientific fact that there are differences between ALL individual things. But we also know, as a personal fact, that for *our own purposes,* there may be no practical difference. As in using any other tool, you must experiment with the **index numbers** to find out how to use them.

Look behind the Words

Here's why we need **index numbers**: once we learn to smile or frown at any particular label, we tend to be almost blind to the things behind the label. From then on, we accept or reject them on a basis of their labels. We do not look at the individual things. We don't think we need to. We do not try to see how they work or why some people like or dislike them. We do not try to increase our understanding of them or try to find out if more knowledge would give us more insight.

Let Mark Twain tell you how people learned to react to his cigars—and how they lost all ability to survey that territory:

People who claim to know say that I smoke the worst cigars in the world. They bring their own cigars when they come to my house. They betray an unmanly terror when I offer them a cigar; they tell lies and hurry away to meet engagements which they have not made when they are threatened with the hospitalities of my box. Now then, observe what superstition, assisted by a man's reputation, can do.

I was to have twelve personal friends to supper one night. One of them was as notorious for costly and elegant cigars as I was for cheap and devilish ones. I called at his house and when no one was looking borrowed a double handful of his very choicest; cigars which cost him forty cents apiece and bore red-and-gold labels in sign of their nobility. I removed the labels and put the cigars into a box with my favorite brand on it—a brand which those people all knew, and which cowed them as men are cowed by an epidemic.

They took these cigars when offered at the end of the supper, and lit them and sternly struggled with them—in dreary silence, for hilarity died when the fell brand came into view and started around—but their fortitude held for a short time only; then they made excuses and filed out, treading on one another's heels with indecent eagerness; and in the morning when I went out to observe results the cigars lay all between the front door and the gate. All except one—that one lay in the plate of the man from whom I had cabbaged the lot. One or two whiffs was all he could stand. He told me afterward that some day I would get shot for giving people that kind of cigars to smoke.*

In this prank of Mark Twain's, we find illustrated one of the differences between sane and insane behavior. The guests reacted to the fixed ideas in their heads and to the misleading

* From Mark Twain, "Concerning Tobacco," *What Is Man?* New York: Harper & Brothers, 1917. Reprinted by permission.

FOUNTAIN PEN$_1$ IS NOT FOUNTAIN PEN$_2$

"Bad one?"

labels they saw—*not to the actual cigars they were puffing.* In this changing world about which we have incomplete knowledge, *sane thinking demands that we base our actions on a survey of the territory rather than a survey of our mind.*

Sanity consists in making adequate maps of the territory. People who are locked up in mental hospitals have the habit of projecting onto the territory the verbal maps they cook up in their heads. They are unable to open their eyes and minds and observe clearly what is before them. They think they know what things are like without checking. What they *think they know blocks them from evaluating sanely.*

The Snap Judgment

Just as a letter sorter in the post office quickly and without any question puts local mail in one bag and out-of-town mail in another, so we in an automatic and unreflective way tend to sort out things on a basis of their labels without even trying to observe **thing**$_1$, **thing**$_2$, **thing**$_3$, etc., behind these labels. That automatic response is fine for the job of post-office letter sorting. But it is not the kind of thinking that enables us to produce mature judgments in this complex world about which we receive so much misinformation. Only open eyes and open minds will mature us and make real human beings out of us.

The snap-judgment attitude with its dogmatic certainty is a disgrace to a human being. A jackass or a fish is not capable of much reflective thought. They are not able to use their brains over a period of years to mature their attitudes. We humans can mature our thinking if we try. But most people have been trained in such jackass methods of thinking that they seldom learn to use their magnificent brains in anything approaching a magnificent way.

To Sum Up

We live in a world where no two things are identical. But we have thinking habits that often mislead us into assuming that two things labeled by the same name are identical. The **index numbers** will help us think in terms of individual things. For mature thinking, we must be aware of both the similarities and the differences between things that are labeled by the same name.

The **index numbers** will remind us of the dangers of generalizing or thinking in terms of averages. We know that no matter how accurate our average picture or generalization is, we do not know whether it applies to any given individual until we survey the territory and get acquainted with $\mathbf{man_1}$ or $\mathbf{thing_1}$—the particular individual.

Tool No. 5: THE WHEN INDEX

8

Keeping Up-to-date

The world rolls; the circumstances vary every hour.
RALPH WALDO EMERSON

In our fast-moving world it is important that we stay on our toes to avoid being surprised by changed conditions. A doctor was awakened in the middle of the night by a phone call from a man for whom he had done some medical work a few years before.

"Doctor," said the excited man, "please come over right away. My wife is in great pain and I'm sure it's her appendix."

"Well, now," replied the doctor, "I don't think that's it. I'll drop around the first thing in the morning. Don't worry. It's probably just indigestion."

"But, doctor, you've got to come right now. I'm positive it's appendicitis," protested the alarmed husband.

"Oh come, Mr. Johnson," the doctor said somewhat irritably. "I took out your wife's appendix almost two years ago. You know as well as I do that that couldn't be it."

"That's true enough," said the husband. "But I've got a different wife."

The doctor assumed that Mr. Johnson's wife of two years ago was the same person as Mr. Johnson's wife on the night of the call. In this case, of course, his assumption was a normal one that anyone might make. But when we come to important matters on which we risk our health, financial security, and happiness, we cannot afford mistakes. If we want to live as worth-while a life as possible, we must try to achieve a .980 average in batting out adequate maps. This will be impossible if we have not developed a deep-down feeling of the way *words* do not change but the *things* represented by our words are constantly changing.

Some things change slowly; some very rapidly. Some things within a year's time will change in important ways; others during this time will undergo only minute changes that are insignificant for our purposes. But whether changes are fast or slow, large or small, **so far as I know** we live in a world where all things are processes.

Think of the various ways we human beings change as the years saunter by. We start out as a fertilized ovum with all our needs supplied. At birth we are ruthlessly evicted without even any clothes or teeth. We try to make the best of this bad situation, and slowly and with much confusion we gradually learn to walk, to talk, and not to pull the tails of big dogs too hard. We keep growing taller and wider, get through various schools, and eventually get started making money or making babies or both. We stop growing taller, but more often than not keep growing wider. Wrinkles and double chins appear, and the hair that does not fall out frequently turns gray. The gallant

ALL THINGS CHANGE

"I'm bringing a surprise home, dear. Remember Lamar, that great, big, handsome he-man you're always talking about, the one you could have married instead of me . . . ?"

husband will stoutly maintain that his wife is just as beautiful as the day he married her—but he will admit that it takes her longer.

From the time we are one minute old to the time we die, the things we like to do and the skills with which we do them constantly change. The foods we enjoy, the sensations we like, and the state of our blood pressure will shift from time to time. What can be one man's meat in one year may be his poison the next. Not only ourselves but the things around us are constantly shifting. The stock market, the weather, the grass on the front lawn, and the rattles of the family car keep changing from time to time.

The North Star

You have probably heard the phrase, "As constant as the North Star." But a close look shows nothing but change. The North Star actually goes around in a circle (from our point of view) and *is due north only twice a day.* And, as if this inconstancy were not enough, the star we call the "North Star" changes over a period of years. When the Egyptians built the Great Pyramids, Alpha Draconis was the North Star. Today it is Polaris. Twelve thousand years from now, Vega in the constellation Lyra will be the North Star. Shakespeare assumed too much when he wrote:

> But I am constant as the Northern star,
> Of whose true, fixed, and resting quality,
> There is no fellow in the firmament.

There are two platinum-iridium meter bars maintained by the Bureau of Standards in Washington to act as master pat-

"Relax! I know this road perfectly! I've been driving it all my life!!"

terns for our yardsticks. Every possible effort is made to prevent changes from taking place in these meter bars. They are kept in a vault and used only about once every five years.

But even these meter bars are not changeless. All things are made up of atoms whose tiny electrons move over 100,000 miles each second. That is a distance of over four times around the earth! What appears to our fingers and eyes as something solid is, on the atomic level, a mad dance of particles constantly knocking each other billions of times per second in a chaos of confusion and unpredictability.

On the atomic level, nothing is the same from one split second to another split second—there is nothing but motion, change, dynamism. Frequently the atoms on the outside of an object will leave the object and escape into the air or into adjacent matter. For example, when a block of lead is put on top of a block of gold, some of the gold atoms will jump in the lead and some of the lead atoms will be found knocking about in the gold.

And so even our meter bars, with all precautions taken to prevent change, will manage to slip a few changes over on us. The loss of a few atoms each year does not keep them from being useful to the Bureau of Standards—but it does qualify them as a rather phlegmatic brother of all other things in the world that constantly change.

Our Maps Can Become Obsolete

On his first trip to the Florida Keys before the war, a New York lawyer spent a delightful day fishing with an old, native, sponge fisherman named Edwards. Noticing how the old-

THE MODES OF YESTERDAY MAY BE THE LAUGHS OF TODAY

"The next thing they'll be doing. . . ."

timer's skin had been browned and wrinkled by the tropical sun, the lawyer said,

"Edwards, would you mind telling me how old you are?"

"Not a bit," he said. "I'm sixty-eight."

Recently this lawyer was again visiting southern Florida and he decided to see if Edwards was still around to take him fishing. He found Edwards sitting on a pier mending some mullet nets. The Florida sun and wind had put a few more wrinkles in Edwards' face, but otherwise the lawyer noticed very little change. After they had been trolling for some time among the islands, he asked the old man how old he was now.

"I'm sixty-eight," was the prompt reply.

"But you said you were sixty-eight when I was here seven years ago," cross-examined the lawyer. "How do you explain that?"

"Explain it? There ain't nothing to explain. Do you think I'm the kind of feller who would be telling you one thing one day and something else the next?"

Unfortunately it is often necessary to tell people one thing one day and something else the next. We change and the world changes. This complicates our attempts to maintain a stock of adequate verbal maps. Just as a portrait photographer has trouble taking a picture of a child who will not keep still, so we have trouble keeping track of a world that will not stand still.

Alfred North Whitehead said, "Knowledge keeps no better than fish." The 1946 edition of the *Encyclopaedia Britannica* has an article on uranium that says: "Its [uranium's] chief use at the present time is in the ceramic industry. . . ." The atomic bomb has made this verbal map as dead as a dodo!

Even if we did know ALL about something today, changes in the terrain may make our verbal maps obsolete tomorrow. We cannot survey the territory once and for all. We must keep our eyes open and our minds open in order to recognize important changes. The facts of yesterday may be the fictions of today.

Living People with Dead Knowledge

"Old age," said Montaigne, "plants more wrinkles in the mind than in the face." A young mind strives continuously to mature its verbal maps. An old mind tries to defend its verbal maps from any change whatsoever. Whether you have a young or an old mind cannot be told by looking at your birth certificate. Some people in their eighties have younger minds than many people in their teens.

"This old age ought not to creep on a human mind," said Emerson. "In nature every moment is new; the past is always swallowed and forgotten; the coming only is sacred. . . . People wish to be settled; only as far as they are unsettled is there any hope for them."

The six **tools for thinking** help us stay "young in spirit" regardless of the number of candles that belong on our birthday cake.

The When Index (or Date)

You "know" you live in a changing world, but how are you going *to act as if you know it*? The **tool for thinking** that will enable you to reflect this principle in your everyday life is the **when index,** or the date. Webster defines an index as an indi-

THE DATE MAKES A DIFFERENCE

"Then I picked her up and whisked her away. This was a good twenty years ago, of course. . . ."

cator, or pointer. The **when index** simply points out WHEN the territory was surveyed.

For the next few months, while you are getting familiar with the application of this tool, deliberately add the date to whatever you talk about: The **U. S. government** *(today)*. **Your mother** *(1930)*. **Your car** *(next year)*. **Your business** *(1964)*.

Whether a given statement is true or false will often depend upon the date. Many futile arguments take place when people omit the **when index:**

MR. A: "Beaver Lodge is a wonderful place. The food is fine. The fishing is good. I don't know why you don't like it."

MR. B: "Why, I swear I don't see how you can stand that place. If that's what you call good food—I'll bet some hog swills are better. And the fishing—I could see them, but they wouldn't bite for anything."

The argument went back and forth, the tempers up and up, and the nasty remarks lower and lower without reaching any agreement. Too bad these two didn't realize that Mr. A was talking about **Beaver Lodge** *(1960)* and Mr. B. was talking about **Beaver Lodge** *(1964)*. Then they might have realized that *both of their maps were adequate provided they were time stamped.*

Since we live in a changing world, we must always be willing to resurvey the territory in order to make our maps reflect the way things are now and not just the way they were last year. Let the historians treasure the out-of-date knowledge—it's their business. It's our business to have in stock the most up-to-date maps that will always give us predictability in our thinking.

The Tools Can Be Misused

Like any tool, the technique of dating can be mishandled. We must not go to the opposite extreme and assume that everything has changed in ways important to us and that the verbal maps of last year are of no use today. We cannot say, "Well, rattlesnakes used to bite people but I understand that absolutely everything is guaranteed to change. I'll just pick up this one."

It is as stupid to assume that things have changed as it is to assume that things have not changed. A fool would be no better off with these **tools for thinking** than he would be without them. Using them requires discrimination and the application of your intelligence. "The individual's own good (or bad) judgment is the guide," said John Dewey. "There is no label, on any given idea or principle, that says automatically, 'Use me in this situation'—as the magic cakes of Alice in Wonderland were inscribed 'Eat me.' The thinker has to decide, to choose; and there is always a risk, so that the prudent thinker selects warily—subject, that is, to confirmation or frustration by later events." *

You must test the **tools for thinking** in your everyday life to find out what they will do for you. You must try them out as you would try out a new gadget. Like all tools, they have limitations. They cannot be used blindly. It takes practice and perseverance to learn what these principles will do for you in your own thinking. Advice, when presented in a book, sounds like "old stuff" and, of course, it is. "Education," said Ruskin,

* From *How We Think* by John Dewey. Reprinted by special permission of D. C. Heath and Company, Boston, Mass.

THOUGH WE LIVE IN A CHANGING WORLD, WE MUST NOT BLINDLY ASSUME THAT EVERYTHING WILL CHANGE IN WAYS IMPORTANT TO US

" 'We don't need to insulate the house,' says he, 'we'll never have another winter like the last one.' "

"does not mean teaching people what they do not know. It means teaching them to behave as they do not behave."

A Great Man and a Great Problem

Albert Einstein was, with Mahatma Ghandi, one of the world's greatest pacifists. Einstein felt that World War I was mainly fought for certain economic reasons, and it did not make much sense to him for a lot of people to get killed just to help a few people get richer. According to this view, such wars are fought under the guise of protecting the national honor. However, when we scratch under the surface, we will find rivalry for colonial possessions and the desire of some businessmen to have their foreign investments protected even if it means that many of their countrymen must die in war.

For many years Einstein taught young people to refuse to serve in any war and to oppose all armaments—even for defense. When one country arms for defense, surrounding countries do likewise. The "defense" programs snowball larger and larger until everyone is ready for war.

As late as the spring of 1931, Einstein maintained this view At that time a group of American clergymen announced they would take no part in future wars even if their government claimed that it was for the defense of the United States. Einstein wrote regarding this manifesto of the clergymen:

> It is a gratifying revelation of the temper of the American clergy that fifty-four per cent of those who answered the questionnaire should have indicated their purpose not to participate in any future war. Only such a radical position can be of help to the world, since the government of each nation is bound to present every war as a war of defense.*

* Reprinted by permission.

However, once having taken his stand in favor of the principle of pacifism, Einstein did not become blind to the facts of this changing world. The things he observed in Germany gradually convinced him that his verbal maps, while adequate for World War I, were not appropriate for the coming World War II. He saw about him a group of fanatics under Hitler who were singing *Deutschland über Alles,* and who were rapidly developing insane methods of thinking: *Wir denken mit unserem Blut*—"We think with our blood." The Nazis showed no respect for freedom of speech, individual liberty, or any other human rights. They were willing to use any amount of terror or force to make the Nazis rulers of the world.

Einstein felt that his pacifist maps no longer fitted the changing conditions. Now, a narrow or consistent man would have stuck by his principles; a consistent man wouldn't be caught changing his mind. He would say, if something is true, it's true; and he would explain away the facts before his eyes. A consistent man would foolishly feel, "If I change my mind, that will be like admitting I've been wrong all these years."

But Einstein, like all mature people, was more interested in having adequate verbal maps than in maintaining a foolish consistency. In the latter part of 1931, a group of Belgian pacifist youths, realizing that Germany was preparing for war, turned to Einstein for advice. The principles they had adopted made them oppose all armaments and military training, but they did not want their country to be defenseless when Germany struck. They were in a dilemma and wanted Einstein's opinion because they had confidence in his integrity and intelligence. He had been living in Germany, and he would have had a good opportunity to survey the territory.

THE TOOLS FOR THINKING CAN PREVENT FIGHTS

"Doris!! You have callers!!!"

When Einstein replied to them, he renounced the pacifist principles that he had spent years of his life building up and defending. When the situation changed, he was willing to change his verbal maps. He was not so blinded by his principles that he couldn't keep them useful. As a scientist, his ideal is straight thinking—not strait-laced thinking.

When Einstein came to the United States in 1932, some women's clubs tried to prevent his immigration on the grounds that he was a "pacifist." But their maps no longer represented the territory. **Einstein**(*January, 1931*) acted in ways that are called pacifist, but **Einstein**(*January, 1932*) had changed. And it is a part of history that **Einstein**(*August 2, 1939*) addressed a letter to President Roosevelt which began:

> Some recent work by E. Fermi and L. Szilard which has been communicated to me in manuscript leads me to expect that the element Uranium may be turned into a new and important source of energy in the immediate future. . . . A single bomb of this type . . . exploded in a port . . . might very well destroy the whole port, together with the surrounding territory. . . .*

A Foolish Consistency

How can we hope to be consistent and never change our minds about things when:

1. Our knowledge is not complete, and
2. The rapidly changing conditions of this modern world from time to time make obsolete even the best maps.

"A foolish consistency," said Emerson, "is the hobgoblin of little minds, adored by little statesmen and philosophers and

* Reprinted by permission.

"Remember that cute little puppy you tried to buy from the Stuarts? They gave him to you today."

divines. With consistency a great soul has simply nothing to do. He may as well concern himself with his shadow on the wall. Speak what you think now in hard words and to-morrow speak what to-morrow thinks in hard words again, though it contradict every thing you said to-day.—'Ah, so you shall be sure to be misunderstood.'—Is it so bad then to be misunderstood? Pythagoras was misunderstood, and Socrates, and Jesus, and Luther, and Copernicus, and Galileo, and Newton, and every pure and wise spirit that ever took flesh. To be great is to be misunderstood."

That is the way Emerson felt toward people who latch on to some "eternal principle" and hold to it no matter what. Walt Whitman expressed himself rather clearly: "Do I contradict myself? Very well, then I contradict myself."

This business of separating the wisdom of the past from the out-of-date ideas, prejudices, humbugs, and bunk that accumulate is beyond a doubt one of the toughest and yet one of the most important things we must do. No one of us is ever entirely right in sorting the sheep from the goats. But the better we do this job of keeping our knowledge up to date, the more successful and the happier we will be.

To Sum Up

When we date our verbal maps, we remind ourselves that our heads are crammed full of what Robert Hutchins called, "rapidly aging facts." "Many a man fails to become a thinker," declared Nietzsche, "for the sole reason that his memory is too good." Dating our maps will help us keep our old knowledge from blocking new learning.

Since reality is constantly washing its face, we must remember occasionally to scrub up our verbal maps, too. The date on a map reminds us that this is the way the territory was when it was surveyed. Whether the map is still adequate at a later date *cannot be told by examining the map. We can tell only by checking the territory of today.*

As the world rolls, we must recheck our verbal maps. As the circumstances vary, so our maps must vary if they are to be useful guides—if they are to have predictability. It is silly to embalm our verbal maps in a changing and jet-propelled world. It is just plain stupid to be "true" to our ideas when they are no longer "true" to us.

Tool No. 6: THE WHERE INDEX

9

Marking the Spot

To a mouse, cheese is cheese. That is why mousetraps are effective.*

WENDELL JOHNSON

In the past five chapters we have discussed five characteristics of our world that make it difficult for us to make adequate verbal maps. Do you remember which **tools for thinking** help us meet these pitfalls to straight thinking?

1. Since it is impossible for us to know ALL about anything, we never have ALL the facts before us when making a decision.
2. Things are not quite so clear-cut as the verbal maps we make. Nothing is pure black or pure white. It is necessary for us to survey the territory thoroughly to find out to what extent it has the characteristic in which we are interested.
3. We have minds that subtly twist things to fit in with our personal interests.

* From *People in Quandaries* by Wendell Johnson. Copyright, 1946. Reprinted by permission of Harper & Brothers.

4. No two things in this world are absolutely identical, and sometimes we are misled when we suppose that two things will act alike because they have the same name.
5. Things have the annoying habit of changing from time to time in ways that frequently make our verbal maps out of date.

We are now ready to take up the last of our **tools for thinking.**

Environmental Differences

WHERE a thing is used often makes a lot of difference. The costume department of one of the larger Hollywood studios submitted sketches of a rather revealing gown to censors for approval before shooting. "The attached gown will be all right," came back the reply, "if it's an evening gown to be used in a night-club scene—but if it's a nightgown to be used in the bedroom scene, it's definitely out." In other words, **gown**$_1$*(in a night club)* has a different effect from **gown**$_1$*(in a bedroom)*—the difference being WHERE it is used.

We come now to the third of our **indexes**: the **where index.** Like the **what** and **when indexes,** the **where index** also helps us to avoid being tripped up by differences. You will recall that the **what index** says to us: "You shouldn't expect two things to act alike just because they are called by the same name or even because they look alike. Since no two things in this world are absolutely identical, you may get stuck by one of the differences. The **index numbers** should remind you of differences." The **when index** says: "Don't blindly assume that things are exactly as they used to be—or you may be fooled."

WHERE YOU ARE MAKES A DIFFERENCE

"Delicious!"

"I expect to die someday, but if you think for a minute it's gonna be on a fish bone. . . ."

Now the **where index** says to us: "Any particular person or thing may act differently when put in a new place—or a new situation, a new environment, under new circumstances, or under new conditions." Although for convenience we are calling it the **where index,** actually we're going to use it in a little broader sense than the word "where" implies. It could be called the "environment index." *The where index represents the whole environment surrounding any person or thing, and reminds us that when parts of the environment change, there may be changes in the way* man_1 *or* $thing_1$ *will act.* And, as with all differences, sometimes the changes may be important for our purposes or they may be so slight that we may ignore them.

"The Man Whose Character Was Hit by a Train"

Sometimes a small and apparently insignificant change in our environment can make a great deal of difference in the way we act. Robert M. Yoder illustrated this by a humorous story published in *The Saturday Evening Post:*

> Each day after leaving work at 5:00 o'clock, Windemere Tuttle would toddle into the corner bar for two Martinis. It was always two Martinis because his train to the suburbs left at 5:25, and he didn't dare miss his train. Now Toby Gintle also dropped into the same bar after work—but Toby's train didn't leave until 6:03. By this time he was up to his Fatal Fourth drink, and sometimes he would even stay until the 6:37. He would get home with a load on, fall asleep after dinner, and hence saw little of his wife and four darling children.
>
> Gintle had tried to persuade Tuttle to miss a train with him, but Tuttle could never be tempted. Gintle regarded him with envy as a resolute man who had his life well programed.

DIFFERENT SITUATIONS, CIRCUMSTANCES, OR SURROUNDINGS BRING OUT DIFFERENT ASPECTS OF PEOPLE AND THINGS

WITH A LABOR SURPLUS

WITH A LABOR SHORTAGE

Then Fate took a hand in Gintle's affairs—Fate in the form of those masters of whimsey and irrelevance who make up suburban-train schedules. Gintle's train was moved forward to 5:02. When he had time for a drink, he wore it off sprinting for the train; usually he got home before six o'clock, cold sober. This gave him so much time of evenings that he began inventing games to combat advanced boredom, and so prevalent is boredom that the games earned him $3000 in March alone, and four times that much in Philadelphia. Gintle is now held up as a model of industry and self-control.

As for Windemere Tuttle, you can find him almost any night, hung on a bar like a coat thrown over a chair, telling some stranger that life is a riddle in double talk. For they changed Windemere's train to 6:07, and at his moderate pace of nine minutes to the Martini, Windemere has become one of the town's worst lushes.*

When we say this with **indexes,** we find that good husband **Windemere Tuttle**(*with suburban train leaving at 5:25*) acts differently from bar-fly **Windemere Tuttle**(*with suburban train leaving at 6:07*). And pie-eyed **Toby Gintle**(*whose train left at 6:03*) acts differently from smart **Toby Gintle**(*whose train leaves at 5:02*).

When any person or thing is moved to a new place or put in a new situation, there may be significant changes in the things that interact with them, such as the attitudes of people, the temperature, the humidity, atmospheric pressure, amount of light and dark, the pollen count of the air, and many other things. For example, when a person with a certain type of allergy leaves a place that is relatively pollen free and goes into

* From "The Story of Two-Drink Tuttle, Whose Character Was Hit by a Train," by Robert M. Yoder. Reprinted with the kind permission of the author and the Curtis Publishing Company. Copyright, 1948.

PEOPLE ACT DIFFERENTLY IN DIFFERENT PLACES AND SITUATIONS

"Then he received the Distinguished Service Medal. Bravery in face of enemy fire."

a place where there is much pollen in the air, he will change from a well person to an extremely sick person.

The Where Index

Everything that exists, exists at a specific place under specific circumstances. Any verbal map that tries to represent the territory as completely as possible should include the **where index.** The **where index** is simply information added to your verbal map that tells the location or the important environmental factors that may influence the person or thing you are talking about.

The **where index** will remind you that any person or thing may act differently in a different situation. **Chair**$_1$ *(in your living room)* will not act the same as **chair**$_1$ *(kept in a damp basement)*. Whether **chair**$_1$ stays in good condition or collapses with your dignity will depend on WHERE it is kept.

You know that your **car radio** *(out in the open)* does not sound the same as your **car radio** *(going under a steel bridge)*. It acts differently in different places.

Suppose we pack a picnic lunch and go out to Surprise Lake for a day's fishing. But just after we get to the lake, the clouds roll up and a steady rain throws a wet blanket on our party. Since it looks pretty dreary, we quickly get back in the car and travel home with glum thoughts of the big fish we might have caught that day.

We get home about noon and spread our picnic lunch out on the dining-room table. The picnic lunch on the dining-room table tastes pretty flat. It lacks the "tang" that the same picnic lunch would have had after a morning of fishing at Surprise

CAR$_1$ (*left in sun*)
IS NOT LIKE
CAR$_1$ (*left in shade*)

1

2

3

Ted Key

Lake. In other words, **picnic lunch$_1$** *(at Surprise Lake)* is not **picnic lunch$_1$** *(on our dining-room table)*. The **what index** tells us that **picnic lunch$_1$** is **picnic lunch$_1$**, but the **where index** reminds us that **picnic lunch$_1$** may taste differently to us in different places.

Cheese Is Cheese

Wendell Johnson said, "To a mouse, cheese is cheese. That is why mousetraps are effective." **Cheese** *(in a mousetrap)* is not the same as **cheese** *(on the pantry shelf)*. If a human being wants to have a brain rating of more than one mouse power, he needs the **indexes.**

Play a game with yourself. Take out your watch and time yourself for one minute: see how many people and things you can think of that act differently when put into different situations. If, in one minute's time, you can think of ten different things and one or more ways in which they will act differently in a new environment, you are doing fine.

As a starter, consider your watch. Your **watch** *(in your hand)* may act differently from your **watch** *(under water)*.

To Sum Up

THE THREE INDEXES IN REVIEW

The **What Index** consists of numbers which remind us that there are no two things in this world that are alike, and that we must keep our eyes open for differences that make a difference.

The **When Index,** or date, reminds us that conditions in this world change from time to time and the verbal maps that were quite adequate yesterday may mislead us tomorrow.

The **Where Index** reminds us that any given person or thing may act differently when moved to a different place or placed in new circumstances.

A person who **indexes** is able to keep an open mind with regard to new things. For example, I had never liked any eggplant I had eaten. After trying it a few times, it's easy for a person to generalize, "I don't like eggplant," and from then on say, "No, thank you." But a person who thinks in terms of indexed eggplant will realize that eggplant IS NOT eggplant —that is, **eggplant**(*fixed in new and different ways*) may seem different from **eggplant** (*the unpleasant remembrance of past eggplant*).

The other day my wife served some eggplant that I found delicious. I could hardly believe it. I suspected that it was impossible. If I had been sure that eggplant is eggplant, I would have "known" in advance that I would not like it. With a closed mind, I would have missed something worth while. Perhaps someday I'll find that although I have not liked **$okra_1$, $okra_2$, $okra_3$,** etc., some **$okra_{56}$** just hits the spot.

To avoid being misled by the past, it's a good idea to **index** all your experiences. "One should be careful," observed Mark Twain, "to get out of an experience only the wisdom that is in it—and stop there; lest we be like the cat that sits down on the hot stove lid. She will never sit down on a hot stove lid again —and that's well; but also she will never sit down on a cold one any more."

10

The Tools in a Nutshell

I keep six honest serving-men
  (They taught me all I knew);
Their names are WHAT and WHY and WHEN
  And HOW and WHERE and WHO.

RUDYARD KIPLING

We have now put six sharp tools in our mental toolbox. They are:

1. **So Far As I Know**
2. **Up to a Point**
3. **To Me**
4. **The What Index**
5. **The When Index**
6. **The Where Index**

We must now learn how to make these tools as useful as possible in our everyday lives. The **tools for thinking** appear simple when described, but, like the golden rule, they have far-reaching consequences when we learn to apply them consistently in action.

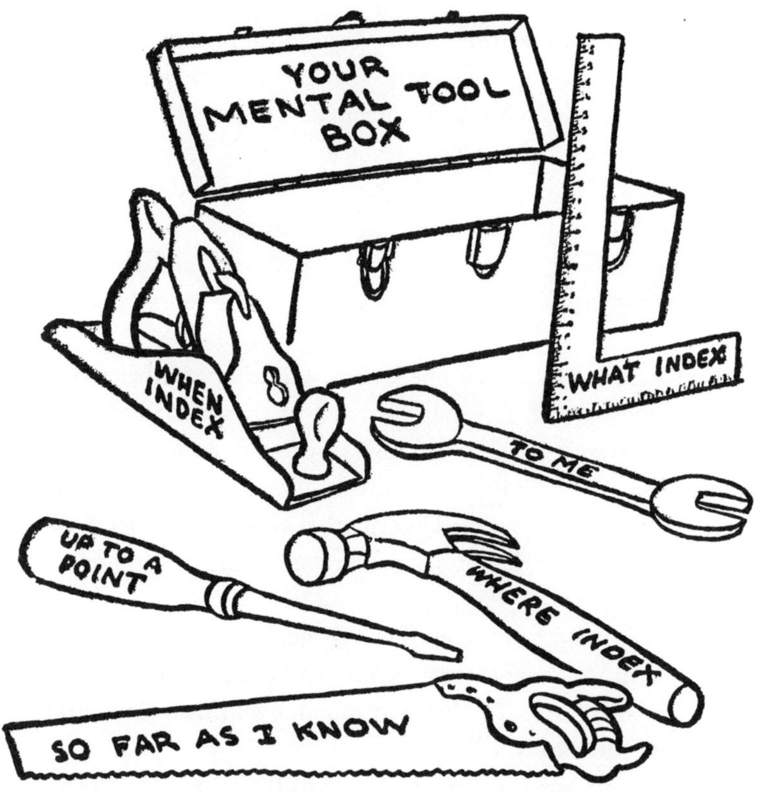

Learning to use the **tools for thinking** requires at least as much effort as learning to use the tools in a carpenter's tool chest. The fact that you have seen saws and hammers as far back as you can remember, and even handled them some yourself, does not mean that you are able to use them in a workmanlike and effective manner. Only practice will develop skill. And remember: it is impossible for you to learn what you think you already know.

Look for the System

A system makes learning easy. You will find that the **tools for thinking** make up a neat little system. In a system the parts are interrelated—each implies other parts. You will find that sometimes several of the tools seem to overlap. In certain situations two of the tools can be used to do approximately the same work in your thinking. *When you begin to see how the* **tools for thinking** *are systematically connected and overlapping, then you will know that you are beginning to understand them.*

You will find that each one makes you think of other tools If this were not so, it would be hard to translate them into action in your everyday thinking. Stray, unrelated bits of knowledge are likely to be forgotten soon, so begin to observe how one tool leads you to think of other tools, and notice how frequently some of the tools are interchangeable in their functions.

Remember these are tools. There is no ONE set way to use any of them. And remember—what you get out of them is not up to the tools—it is strictly up to you and your own cleverness in putting them to work.

Every effort has been made to present these **tools for thinking** in a simple way. This has been designed as a handbook which can be read and absorbed as painlessly as possible. There is a danger that it has been made so simple it will be ignored by many people who like more scholarly presentations.

The purpose of the **tools for thinking** is to enable everyone to achieve mature thinking habits. Without these **tools for thinking** and the philosophy of thinking in terms of verbal

WHY TRUTH IS SO HARD TO REACH

maps, *it is much more difficult to learn the basic premises of straight thinking.*

Read This Book Several Times

If you will read this book a second time, you will find that you get much more out of it than on the first reading. The first reading serves only to break the ice. On the second reading it really sinks in. Even on further readings you will find that you notice new things and develop new insights.

If you bought a book on contract bridge, you would not expect it to make you a bridge expert overnight. You might find that your first attempts at counting honor tricks, applying the formulas for bidding, and using the Blackwood slam convention, would perhaps make you play a slower game than usual. In a well-thought-out system, such as the Culbertson, the rules are clear-cut and most of the problems you will meet are covered by various principles. But when you actually get involved in a bridge game, there are all sorts of distractions, tensions, and unexpected complications. The rules seem simple enough—the difficulty is in remembering when to apply a particular rule. The same thing applies to using the **tools for thinking.** It takes practice, practice, and more practice before you can apply ANY rules or ANY principles effectively.

You will find the outline on the next page useful in checking your knowledge of these tools:

THE SIX TOOLS FOR THINKING

Why It's Difficult to Make Adequate Verbal Maps	*Tools That Can Help Us*	*How the Tools Help Us*
No one knows ALL about anything, and a single overlooked fact may force us to revise our verbal maps.	SO FAR AS I KNOW	This tool reminds us of our incomplete knowledge and helps us keep an open mind toward new evidence.
Most things in this world are not pure black or pure white; they range from ALL to NONE; from zero to 100 per cent. Our EITHER-OR habits of thinking often mislead us.	UP TO A POINT	This tool reminds us of the degree nature of things; it makes us survey the territory to find out up to what point things have the characteristic we are interested in.
The way we feel about things depends on our own particular heredity, training, experiences, and personal interests. Each of us has his own particular brand of Mental One-sidedness.	TO ME	**To me** reminds us that no one sees things from all points of view. **To me** warns us that when we make judgments, we are talking about our own tastes and standards just as much as we are talking about things outside of us.
No two things in this world are identical in ALL respects. We frequently make mistakes by assuming that all things called by the same name will act the same.	THE WHAT INDEX: Man$_1$ IS NOT man$_2$. Thing$_1$ IS NOT thing$_2$.	Index numbers remind us that we can be misled by group words and averages. They help us watch for differences that make a difference.
We live in a process world in which ALL things are changing. The facts of yesterday may be the fictions of today.	THE WHEN INDEX: Henry Jones *(1950)* IS NOT Henry Jones *(1964)*	The when index reminds us that this was the way things were when the territory was surveyed and that the march of time may have made our verbal maps out of date.
Any particular person or thing may act differently when put in new circumstances. Nothing exists in isolation; everything is affected by surrounding conditions.	THE WHERE INDEX: Shark$_1$ *(in water)* IS NOT Shark$_1$ *(on land)*	The where index will remind us to be on the lookout for changes in behavior when man$_1$ or thing$_1$ is placed in a different environment.

Part III

USING THE TOOLS IN EVERYDAY LIFE

The rest of this book will show you how to apply the **tools for thinking** in some of the most important areas of your life. In the next five chapters you will learn how they can help you:

1. Get along better with other people.
2. Build a happier marriage.
3. Achieve success in business.
4. Find causes for things that worry you.
5. Build a world free from wars and want.

11

Getting Along with People

They will tell you to try to prove you are right: I tell you to try to prove you are wrong.

LOUIS PASTEUR

Unless you are a hermit, much of your happiness and success depend upon:

1. How well you are able to reach agreement with people.
2. How well you are able to get along with people *whether or not you agree with them.*

If you were sure that from now on you would deal only with people you like who would never disagree with you, you might skip this chapter. But if you are not a hermit or a little dictator surrounded by "yes men," you will find the **tools for thinking** useful in helping you get along with people as you find them in this scrambled world of ours.

These chapters showing how to use the tools are only suggestive. In each chapter I have only been able to give an example of how you may start applying the **tools for thinking** in your personal affairs. You should find the process of applying them as interesting as the results are profitable. They may turn failure into success, depending upon how well you use this new pathway to effective thinking.

Tool No. 1: So Far As I Know

No argument can be settled when one or both parties blow up emotionally. One of the best ways I have ever found to turn aside wrath is to add **so far as I know** to my verbal maps. Most people will not mind your expressing an opinion that is different from theirs as long as you use **so far as I know** to indicate that your opinion is based upon your experiences and your evidence, and that you are not pretending to be God's mouthpiece. You have not weakened your position at all by saying "**So far as I know.**" After all, who has a right to say more? In a changing world about which our knowledge is incomplete, no one is able to say the final word.

Look at the results Benjamin Franklin achieved when he dropped the dogmatic attitude. In his *Autobiography,* he attributes much of his success to his adoption of the **so far as I know** attitude:

> I made it a rule to forbear all direct contradiction to the sentiments of others, and all positive assertion of my own. I even forbid myself the use of every word or expression in the language that imported a fixed opinion, such as *certainly, undoubtedly,* etc., and I adopted, instead of them, *I conceive, I apprehend,* or *I imagine* a thing to be so or so, or *it so appears to me at present.*
>
> When another asserted something that I thought an error, I denied myself the pleasure of contradicting him abruptly

and of showing immediately some absurdity in his proposition; and in answering, I began by observing that in certain cases or circumstances his opinion would be right, but in the present case there *appeared* or *seemed* to me some difference, etc. I soon found the advantage of this change in my manner; the conversations I engaged in went on more pleasantly. The modest way in which I proposed my opinions procured them a readier reception and less contradiction; I had less mortification when I was found to be in the wrong, and I more easily prevailed with others to give up their mistakes and join with me when I happened to be in the right.

And this mode, which I at first put on with some violence to natural inclination, became at length so easy, and so habitual to me, that perhaps for these fifty years past no one has ever heard a dogmatical expression escape me. And to this habit (after my character of integrity) I think it principally owing that I had early so much weight with my fellow-citizens when I proposed new institutions, or alterations in the old, and so much influence in public councils when I became a member; for I was but a bad speaker, never eloquent, subject to much hesitation in my choice of words, hardly correct in language, and yet I generally carried my points.

The Hardest Thing to Give, Is In

"Men occasionally stumble over the truth," said Winston Churchill, "but most of them pick themselves up and hurry off as if nothing had happened."

Distasteful as it may be, we must train ourselves to listen with an open mind to the opinions of people whom we dislike heartily. We must not be like the Communist sailor, who, when shown on an atlas that there was no Port of Madrid exclaimed, "Ho, ho, do you think I would believe that damn Capitalist map!"

ONCE WE HAVE ADOPTED A POINT OF VIEW, IT IS DIFFICULT TO BE OPEN-MINDED TOWARD FACTS ON THE OTHER SIDE

"That's not him—Dad wouldn't be seen under that paper!"

We should not shut ourselves off from information simply because we do not like where it comes from. Unpopular persons, magazines, and newspapers are often keen critics and fact-finders that are able to bring out clearly some truth on their side of a question and reveal weaknesses in their opponent's cases. When we refuse to examine their facts and arguments, we often choose ignorance instead of knowledge. "Love your enemies," said Benjamin Franklin, "for they tell you your faults."

Our silly feelings of false pride often make us unable to acknowledge our ignorance and our mistakes. But in a changing world about which we have incomplete knowledge, sometimes the most intelligent things we can say are, "I don't know," and, "I have made a mistake." This attitude will count in our favor. People will be able to say of us, "He (or she) is big enough to admit a mistake." If, instead, we insist upon hanging on to our inadequate maps, we will show that we lack the fairness to be reasonable. People will respect us far more if they know that:

1. We add **so far as I know** to our maps, and
2. We drop a map as soon as it appears to be inadequate.

I have very little confidence in people who are not big enough to admit their mistakes. I have a sneaking suspicion that most of their ideas are simply mistakes they should have outgrown a long time ago.

Tool No. 2: Up to a Point

When we criticize people it is important to tell **up to what point** that criticism is appropriate. Suppose, for example, someone complains that doctors are mercenary and think more of the long green lining their pockets than of the Hippocratic ideal of helping suffering humanity. Such a one-sided verbal map will needlessly antagonize the very doctors he would like to change. He has not told **up to what point** his verbal map represents the territory. His map implies that ALL doctors, everywhere, are that way in every respect.

But if he tries to make his verbal maps represent the territory and indicate, for example, that *certain doctors in certain places* accept "kickbacks" or "bonuses" from medical laboratories and supply houses that sometimes amount to from 25 to 50 per cent of the money their patients pay for eyeglasses, X rays, medical appliances, Wassermann and other tests, then he will find that open-minded members of the medical profession will agree with him. Overstating one's case only causes antagonism. One should be careful not to let his assertions outstrip his facts.

Of course, no one enjoys being criticized. But most people will be fair-minded and listen to criticism if we are careful to make maps that adequately represent the territory. We must avoid making a sweeping condemnation. We must indicate **up to what point** our map covers the individuals in question. By using the tool **up to a point** in our thinking, we can avoid drawing maps that lean too far in one direction.

Tool No. 3: To Me

A Chinese delegate to the United Nations was just leaving the gangplank of his ship at a New York dock. He was immediately surrounded by reporters. One of the questions shot at him was, "What strikes you as the oddest thing about Americans?"

The delegate thought seriously for a moment, then smiled. "I think," he said, "it is the peculiar slant of their eyes."

We live in a world made up of five major skin colors, thousands of religions and philosophies, and a range of customs and mores of amazing diversity. If we are to get along with any people except those in our own group, we must learn to add **to me** to our verbal maps. We must recognize that what seems "right" **to us** may not seem "right" **to other people.**

When the British movie film *The Wicked Lady* was sent to the United States, the American censors objected to the necklines of some of the dresses—there was too much "cleavage." For Americans, the censors said, the necklines are immoral. J. Arthur Rank, England's leading film producer, was unable to understand the situation. "In England," he said, "bosoms aren't sexy!"

A little later Hollywood sent *Her Husband's Affairs* over to England. In this movie, twin beds were shown touching each other. The flabbergasted producers in Hollywood could hardly believe their ears when the English explained that they just couldn't show the picture with the twin beds right together. It was necessary to reshoot that scene with the beds placed one foot apart in order to make it in good moral taste for English audiences.

The bathing suits grandma wore are **to us** good for a hearty laugh. But, as you know, when grandma was a very young girl, it was scandalous for her to uncover her ankles and raise the pants legs all the way to the knees. O. A. Wall, in commenting on proper and improper dress in different parts of the world, wrote:

FEW THINGS ARE THE SAME TO ALL PEOPLE

> Among ourselves, perhaps the first effort of a girl surprised naked would be to hide the sexual parts, but among the Malays a girl or woman would under similar circumstances cover her navel with her hands; and the women of some African tribes wear an apron behind, and if they lose this apron they sit down until another is handed them because it would be very indecent to expose their posteriors to sight, while a bare front is perfectly chaste and proper.
>
> Among Turks, Egyptians and Mohammedans generally the faces of the women must be kept hidden, and a Turkish woman surprised by a man with her face uncovered will, if no other covering is at hand, raise her garments and throw them over her head even if by so doing she exposes her naked body from the bosom down. . . .
>
> In some Arabian tribes modesty requires that the back of the head and hair be kept covered, while in China the foot and leg of a woman must not be exposed to view, and may not even be mentioned in polite society.*

The only way we can get along with people who have a contrasting background is to add **to me** to our verbal maps. We must admit we are fallible humans trying to do the best we can. We must not act as if we alone have the key to the treasury of truth.

Our Judgments Are Self-reflective

When we say, "Jane is an interesting girl," we're talking about ourselves just as much as we are talking about Jane. The way we react to things is partly determined by what is outside us and partly by what is inside us. When we say, "Jane is an interesting girl," we really mean that WE find Jane interesting

* From *Sex and Sex Worship* by O. A. Wall. St. Louis: C. V. Mosby Company, Medical Publishers. Copyright, 1922. Reprinted by permission.

for one or more reasons. That statement gives other people very little information about Jane—it only expresses the way *we feel about her.*

If we hear someone say, "That building is hideous," we must remember that he is expressing his standards and his ideas of architecture just as much as he is talking about the building. That statement simply means he doesn't like the building.

If you ask someone, "Did you like the movie you saw?" and he replies, "Oh, it was a grand movie," remember that he is talking about himself just as much as he is talking about the movie. If both of your tastes are similar, his judgments and opinions will be useful **to you.**

When someone says, "Those clothes are beautiful," he is talking about HIS standards and HIS tastes and what HE is used to. The beauty lies not alone in the clothes; it lies also in the eyes and mind of the person making the judgment.

The tool **to me** will help us become conscious of the way our own nervous system abstracts differently from other nervous systems. All we have the right to say is, "**To me** this is beautiful. **To me** this is bad. **To me** this is fun. **To me** this tastes wonderful. **To me** this is interesting. **To me** this is dull," and so on. We can speak only for ourselves.

It is a rare person who does not use the terms: "proper," "right," or "best," to apply to the way he personally thinks things should be done. A mature thinker recognizes the human equation in knowledge. He lays his cards on the table. By adding **to me** to his verbal maps, he converts his dogmatic and otherwise egocentric maps into inoffensive statements that promote human understanding.

Tool No. 4: The What Index

A retired judge once remarked to one of his friends that during his career on the bench, he had *on the average* done a pretty good job. "Of course," he admitted, "I have sent to the gallows a good many innocent people and have set free a good many guilty people, but I feel on the whole my errors of leniency have been pretty well offset by the times when I was too severe."

From a *statistical* point of view the judge may have averaged out all right—but from an *individual human* point of view there is no such thing as averaging out. It is small comfort to an innocent man about to be hanged to realize that his execution will be balanced out by the mistake of setting a murderer free!

What Is Prejudice?

Prejudice arises when people take a statistical approach to **man**$_1$ or **thing**$_1$. We are prejudiced when we react to labels instead of looking at **man**$_1$ or **thing**$_1$. We are prejudiced when we are content with "averaging out."

All of us carry around in our heads a pack of prejudices. We may be prejudiced against certain races and certain classes. We may be prejudiced against people with immigrant heritages. We have political prejudices, religious prejudices, prejudices against people in other parts of the world and in other parts of our own country, and we can even be prejudiced against people in the next town or in another part of our own town. We can have prejudices about newfangled contraptions, red automobiles, or modern art.

A STATISTICAL AVERAGE MAY NOT COVER MAN_1 OR WOMAN_1

"Are you a—quote—'Vivacious female, intellectual, bored with companions, like soft music, canoeing, laughter, wishes to cut loose from surroundings?' "

We get an unfavorable picture in our heads and then proceed blindly as though that picture were an adequate map to represent ALL people or things that are included under the label. Or we can get a favorable picture in our heads and then blind ourselves to all sorts of unfavorable aspects of **man$_1$** or **thing$_1$**. We ask what a person or thing "is." Then we react to the label. Why bother getting acquainted with the territory—it's too much trouble.

In the February, 1948, issue of *The Atlantic Monthly,* a Jewish person wrote an article explaining why he changed his name. It took thirty days' waiting and cost $60 and had the following effect: *people began to react to HIM and not to his Jewish name.* He said it was like joining the human race when he got rid of the one thing that heaped upon him a smoldering pile of prejudice. He found that with a non-Jewish name people accepted him "as just another guy." They became acquainted with *him* instead of being alienated by a label. He found that by side-stepping the prejudices of a name, he achieved "a sense of freedom as bracing as a good salt wind from the ocean." When people could see *him* rather than their own anti-Jewish prejudices, they liked him. But before he changed his name, their intelligence was stymied by their prejudices toward a label, and they could only respond with the I-don't-want-you-to-work-live-play-near-me attitude.

In Shakespeare's play *Romeo and Juliet,* Juliet cries:

> What's in a name? That which we call a rose
> By any other name would smell as sweet.

But Juliet finds that there is in a name whatever people want to put in it. Until we learn to use the tools for thinking,

WE ARE PREJUDICED WHEN WE REACT TO LABELS INSTEAD OF RESPONDING TO MAN_1

"My family? One-fourth Dutch, one-eighth Irish, one-sixteenth French Huguenot, one thirty-second. . . ."

roses to us just don't smell as sweet under another name. *We find what we are looking for, and we are looking for what is already in our minds.* "Eyes will not see," said Seneca, "when the heart wishes them to be blind. Desire conceals truth, as darkness does the earth." Because of the closed eyes and closed minds that plague all the people some of the time (and some of the people all the time), a rose going under another name may reek to high heaven—**to us.**

The word "prejudice" means to pre-judge. We judge a person by his name or by the labels applied to him. In fact, *we really do not judge the person.* We just show how *we feel about things that are labeled in a certain way.* We close our eyes and act in accordance with the ideas inside our heads. We think we know ALL about the person or thing, and we refuse to check the territory in front of us. As nine-year-old Michael Hobson, son of Laura Hobson (who wrote *Gentlemen's Agreement*), said: "Prejudice is when you decide some fellow's a stinker before you meet him."

Regardless of whether few, many, or most of the people are covered by a generalization, we will meet some who are not. We must observe **man**$_1$ who stands before us in order to act intelligently and fairly toward him.

The **index numbers** can remind us that we do not deal with people-in-general. We deal with individual people and an individual person may or may not fit the average map we have. We must remember that **man**$_1$ is not **man**$_2$, **Democrat**$_1$ is not **Democrat**$_2$, **Republican**$_1$ is not **Republican**$_2$, **Southerner**$_1$ is not **Southerner**$_2$, **New Englander**$_1$ is not **New Englander**$_2$, **Catholic**$_1$ is not **Catholic**$_2$, etc. As Henry van Dyke said, "There is one point in which all men are exactly alike and that

"You on the bear rug."

is that they are all different." By using **index numbers** we can avoid being misled by the stereotyped notions we carry around in our heads.

Tool No. 5: The When Index

In dealing with people, we must remember that although their names do not change, they may act differently with the passing of time. **Susie** *(1960)* may have had many habits that made people call her selfish. **Susie** *(today)* may not have those habits. You cannot simply meet **Susie** *(1960)* and decide she is selfish, then for the rest of your life assume that's the way she is because that's the way she was. Susie may have changed (and, of course, Susie may not have changed). The point is, again, to survey the Susie-territory before you hang a 1960 label on her today.

If we want to react to people as they *are* (rather than to people as they *were*), we must recognize the process factor in knowledge. We must remember with Whitehead that "Knowledge keeps no better than fish."

All of us make missteps. All of us have done mean, selfish, illegal, unworthy, and terrible things. If people make verbal maps of us at such unfortunate times, and then set them in concrete in their minds and refuse to reevaluate us at later times, then we're sunk. When that happens, a person may feel there is no need to try to act better or improve himself. He may feel that his reputation is established, and no matter how he changes, it will not help him because people are not open-minded enough to revise their verbal maps when the territory changes. You can see what unhappiness poor thinking habits

"Remember the kid brother we used to throw quarters to?"

can cause. Clear thinking demands that we use the **when index** to attune ourselves to the possibilities of change.

Tool No. 6: The Where Index

According to words, Mary Williams is Mary Williams. But according to facts, **Mary Williams**(*married to Roger Brown in Boston, Mass.*) is not the same as **Mary Williams**(*married to Tom Smith in Miami, Fla.*). We act differently in different environments and with different people. For example, with some people you usually feel lighthearted and gay, and you get known to them as a clever and witty person. With others, the serious aspect of your personality is brought out.

Suppose two friends of Mary Williams get together:

"Mary is certainly full of the devil. She doesn't have a serious thought in her head."

"We must not be talking about the same person. The Mary I know is quite serious. Her grasp of current affairs is amazing."

"Well, that's not the Mary I'm talking about."

"Mary Williams?"

"Yes, Mary Williams. Lives at the Wingate Apartments."

"I don't know what's the matter. You must not know her very well."

"Why, I've known her for years."

"Well, you certainly aren't much of a judge of character then."

"Well, I like that. I think you're the batty one." (At this point they stop talking about Mary Williams entirely, and inferences and judgments are exchanged that have no relation to the territory.)

THE TOOLS FOR THINKING HELP US
AVOID DISAGREEMENTS

"Why must you always spoil an argument by using the tools for thinking?"

To get along in this world, we need to develop a deep feeling for the way different situations, circumstances, or surroundings bring out different aspects of people and things. The **where index** can help us understand where we might otherwise misunderstand.

To Sum Up

The **tools for thinking** can do a great deal to help you get along with other people. When you say **so far as I know,** you can keep from antagonizing people by your dogmatic assertions. The tool **up to a point** can help you to avoid irritating people needlessly by keeping you from implying "ALL" when "SOME" is more in accordance with the facts. The tool **to me** tells you that your reactions are determined both by what is outside you and your own nervous system. When you use **to me** you admit you're a human being and are not pretending to see things from the cosmic aspect of eternity. By using **index numbers,** you will remember to discriminate *between* individuals and not *against* individuals. No matter how accurate your generalizations and averages are, they do not put the finger on any individual. You must survey the territory to find out if a generalization applies to the **man**$_1$ or **thing**$_1$ you are dealing with. The **when index** will remind you that two verbal maps may seem to contradict each other, but when the date is added both may be found adequate. The **where index** will remind you that people and things act differently in different places.

12

Making Yours a Happy Marriage

> It was a wise man who said that it is important not only to pick the right mate but to *be* the right mate.
>
> DONALD CULROSS PEATTIE

All that has just been said in the last chapter about getting along with people applies as well to getting along in marriage. For after all, marriage is a matter of learning to live with one particular person with whom you have chosen to blend your life.

Meet Mary and John

Let us suppose before they were married Mary and John had learned to use the **tools for thinking** in their everyday affairs. We will, in imagination, follow Mary and John during the first few years of their married life to find out some of the ways they found these **tools for thinking** useful in building a happy marriage.

While Mary and John had been growing up, they had both

had their share of romantic novels, movies, and soap operas. Out of all this, they had developed ideas of what marriage and wives and husbands were like. They looked forward to marriage as a blissful dream. Mary was so beautiful and exciting, and John was so handsome and clever, they were sure that in their marriage they would live happily ever after.

Once they had begun to live together, they realized how incomplete had been their knowledge of each other before they were married. During their courtship, they had thought of each other in terms of ideal pictures. To Mary, John was her particular version of Clark Gable. To John, Mary was the girl of his dreams who was stripped of mortal faults and failings.

They found that before marriage they had been more or less living in a romantic dream world. In a sense, they had married ideals—but now their business was to live with and to love an individual—with all of his and her good and bad points. Before marriage, John had been used to seeing Mary only when she was dressed for a date. When Mary is half-awake in the morning with tousled hair and no make-up, she is not the glamorous sophisticate John had been used to. He had been seeing the show from the point of view of the audience. Now he must get used to glimpses of the backstage aspects as well.

But since John had a mature grasp of the **so-far-as-I-know-now** attitude, he expected in advance that his maps did not represent ALL the territory. He knew there were many factors left out and that he must avoid "disillusionment" when his more adequate survey of the territory let him bring his verbal maps into line with the realities.

Mary's ideal pictures of marriage made her look forward

HIS IDEA OF MARRIAGE

HER IDEA OF MARRIAGE

to being held forever in the arms of her Prince Charming. But John, like other males, enjoyed getting out occasionally with the gang. At first, Mary was disappointed when John wanted to go bowling every Thursday night with the boys and not take her along. He could have taken her, of course, but the other fellows didn't take their wives, and they all liked to make it a stag affair. Mary's verbal maps about marriage had made no provision for this "gang sociability." At first she felt somewhat hurt, but then she realized that it was not that John had changed—it was simply that her verbal maps about men and marriage had not been complete in the first place. Her habit of adding **so far as I know** to her verbal maps helped her meet this problem maturely.

Their desire to understand each other and to make their love increase as the years went by did a great deal to help them pass over with a frown and a smile the many things that come up when two people interlock their lives in the most intimate possible way. After their first child arrived, Mary began to take stock of a woman's lot. And a hard one it seemed **to her.** Out of bed early in the morning to fix breakfast for the man behind the newspaper. After the breakfast dishes have been washed, baby demands his morning bath. When the baby has been bathed and put in his play-pen, there is a house to be swept and dusted. While pausing a moment to decide whether the curtains can go another week before washing, she remembers she had better get to the market soon if she wants to get some fresh vegetables before they are picked over. Putting baby in the buggy (he needed changing again), Mary hurries to the grocery store.

When she gets back it is almost lunchtime. It's too much

IT ALL DEPENDS ON YOUR POINT OF VIEW

bother and fuss to cook a regular meal. She just opens a can of vegetable soup for herself. After taking out a few minutes to admire baby's pink toes, she puts him in his crib for his afternoon nap and sinks into a chair for a short rest. With a start she remembers that baby is down to his last suit and there are no more clean towels in the house. Just as she finishes washing the things needed to get them through the week end, the phone rings. Mary reluctantly tells Janice that since she does not have anyone to leave the baby with, she will have to pass up the bridge party next Tuesday.

By this time Mary begins fixing supper. She thinks how nice it would be to have a day off every now and then. No meals to fix, no house to clean, no baby to interrupt her every few minutes. Everyone in the world except the housewife gets a day off—a woman's work is never done. "It's a man's world," Mary concludes, "Women work for the men, doing the dullest and most routine slave jobs for the longest hours with the shortest pay found anywhere."

But John does not understand what she is talking about. To him it seems that the woman's world is the easier. He has to keep his nose to the grindstone all day in order to make enough money to take care of Mary and the baby. He must get to work every morning exactly on time whether he feels like it or not. All day long he is harassed to death by worrisome telephone calls, complaining customers, and salesmen, in addition to his other problems. His boss likes to get rid of "dead wood" in the organization, and the threat of dismissal always hangs over his head. He feels a heavy responsibility, for he shudders to think what might happen if he lost his job and his weekly salary check stopped coming in. It takes almost every penny

The husband's idea of the wife's day

The wife's idea of the husband's day

he makes just to pay for food, rent, clothing, and taxes, to say nothing of a few luxuries. He thinks how lucky Mary is to be able to stay at home all day without a worry and run things the way she wants rather than having to get to the office at 8:30 every morning and until 5:00 P.M. be a cog in someone else's business. He can't see why Mary thinks going to work in the morning is like going to a country club.

John and Mary have two priceless assets: they are in love, and they are mature people capable of handling life's problems in an adult fashion. They know they must add **so far as I know** and **to me** to their verbal maps to indicate that they are acquainted only with their own side of any situation. They realize that their individual maps do not represent ALL the territory. John and Mary are able to listen to each other's point of view, and thereby develop a deeper understanding of the situation. They are drawn closer together as they realize that each works as a member of a team and that both have their own individual problems which weigh heavily upon their own shoulders, but lightly upon the shoulders of the other. They can explain to each other life as they see it and laugh at the way they have been somewhat blind to the other's point of view. They realize that this is neither a man's world nor a woman's world. It belongs to both men and women, and both must share their part of the work and happiness.

Time-stamping the Maps

John and Mary are used to dating their verbal maps, and they realize that **up to a point** everyone can change. They can change for the better or they can change for the worse. They know it takes time for two people to learn to get along with

FEW THINGS ARE THE SAME TO ALL PERSONS

"What show did you see, children? Did you have a nice nap, Calvin?"

each other every day, every week, every month, every year. They know that it takes as much desire and effort to build a happy marriage as it does to build a successful business. They realize that if they put as much effort into their marriage as they would put into any other important activity, their marriage will be a success. "Marriage is a job," said Kathleen Norris. "Happiness or unhappiness has nothing to do with it. There was never a marriage that could not be made a success, nor a marriage that could not have ended in bitterness and failure." *

They know it takes time for John to work up in the business world to the place where he is comfortable financially and has a feeling of security. It takes time for Mary to learn to prepare the kind of meals they both like and which fit into their family budget. It takes time for them to find friends and activities that will mean the most to them. It takes time to become familiar with things that annoy or please one another. It takes time to achieve sexual adjustment. The habit of dating their verbal maps attunes them to the process factor in their lives.

Drawing the Line

John and Mary realize that marriage is a matter of give-and-take, of trying to adjust to each other and work out compromises that will recognize the points of view of each of them. In marriage as in most anything else, EITHER-OR attitudes are usually inappropriate. The problem is not whether John should go out with the boys or stay at home with Mary. It is

* Reprinted by permission of the author and *The Reader's Digest.* Copyright, 1944.

a problem of where to draw the line: **up to what point** should John and Mary have outside activities.

There is an old saying, "Betwixt two vices every virtue lies." Practically any virtue beyond a certain point becomes a vice. For example, tolerance and open-mindedness are virtues that most of us could use a lot more of. But like most good things, a fool could manage to overdo them. A person can be so open-minded that he becomes empty-minded and changes his opinion under pressure from every new person he meets.

Take the name of any virtue and put the word "too" in front of it, and you will have the name of a vice. Working industriously is an important virtue—**up to a point.** But we can work so hard that we wear ourselves down. We stay tired; we have a bad disposition; we break our health and die early. Sanitation and health measures are important—**up to a point.** But there are a few people who soak all their raw vegetables in peroxide to kill germs. They would not think of eating out because they know that restaurants cannot be depended upon to serve antiseptic food.

In everyday life, as in art, it is important to know where to draw the line. ALL-or-NONE thinking usually gets us into trouble. A person who tried to save all his money for the future would be just as unwise as a person who saved nothing. **Up to a point** we must live happily in the present, and **up to a point** we must try to build for the future. If we draw the line too far either way, we will fail to be as happy as we could have been. Neither the spendthrift nor the miser has a true appreciation of the value of money. And so it would be possible to go on indefinitely trotting out one virtue after another and show

"PERHAPS MORE LIVES ARE RUINED THROUGH INABILITY TO DEAL WITH EVERYDAY COMMON THINGS THAN FOR ANY OTHER REASON"

H. N. Weiman

"Those old good-for-nothing check stubs you kept in that drawer?"

that there is a point beyond which practically any one of them becomes a vice.

Some of the things we regard as vices can in small quantities —**up to some point**—be regarded as virtues. We rightly regard laziness, selfishness, and egotism as despicable vices, but Chesta Holt Fulmer finds in them a formula for being a perfect wife: "Too lazy to quarrel, too selfish to carry a grudge, and too egotistical to be jealous." Said H. L. Mencken: "The way to hold a husband is to keep him a little bit jealous. The way to lose him is to keep him a little bit more jealous."

John and Mary have found the habit of thinking in terms of degrees a basic necessity for achieving a happy marriage. The EITHER-OR and ALL-or-NONE way of thinking can create unnecessary arguments and "insoluble" problems. John and Mary use **up to a point** in their everyday thinking to produce degree maps to fit this degree world.

The Personal Factor

John and Mary are proud of the way they can think maturely about their problems. They see about them many married couples who fuss and feud over matters that to John and Mary are like water rolling off a duck's back. Many conflicts are avoided by using the tool **to me.**

"Perhaps," said Weiman, "more lives are ruined through inability to deal with little everyday common things than for any other reason." The things that break up most couples and cause so much unhappiness usually lack the Cecil B. de Mille touch. They are often such things as disagreements over bedcoverings, the color of neckties, late sleeping or early rising, a liking for reading in bed or a disliking for reading in bed, the

YOUR POINT OF VIEW CAN CHANGE THINGS

"But he's not my Daddy—"

"He's my Mommy."

time of the meals, the choice of perfumes, fluorescent lamps, kind of recreation, and the amount of sex activity.

Since Mary and John know they are different from each other in many ways, they expect that their reactions will not always agree. Some people like to sit up close in the movies; some like to sit in the back. Some people like rooms very warm; others like them much cooler. Some are sensitive to things out of their place; others are not disturbed by any amount of confusion. Some people like fresh air; others are not sensitive to slight odors of staleness or cigarette smoke. Some people like music for its rhythm; others enjoy it for its harmony. Some people like food steaming hot; others will not touch it that way.

We differ in what we find funny: some people like bedroom jokes; some like bathroom jokes—some like both. Some people are disturbed by the slightest criticism, while others will ignore gross insults. Some people go through life demanding "to see the manager"; others, like Mr. Milquetoast, are timid souls. Some people are so allergic to egg protein that they can't eat eggs several days in succession. Some cannot eat an egg at all but are not affected by the amount of egg they would get, for example, in a cake. A few people are so sensitive to tiny amounts of egg that they will become ill after kissing an individual who has eaten egg!

Studies have shown that couples who knew each other for only a few months before marriage had a statistically poorer chance of being happily married than those who went together for several years. An advantage of a long courtship is to help the couple become acquainted with each other's individual tastes and traits.

Man$_1$ is not **man**$_2$; **woman**$_1$ is not **woman**$_2$; **man**$_1$ is not

AVOID ARGUMENTS: MARRY SOMEONE WHO USES THE TOOLS FOR THINKING

". . . and another thing I saw in your diary . . . !"

woman$_1$. John and Mary realize that all people are turned out in molds that are somewhat different. All of us have certain aptitudes and all of us lack some aptitudes. When differences come up, John and Mary are not indignant—they expect differences. They can talk about them rationally and calmly instead of accusing each other of being peculiar or queer. By **indexing** and adding **to me** to their verbal maps, *they laugh at their differences rather than fight out who is "right."* With Mary and John, little acorns of disagreement do not grow into oaks of unhappiness and divorce.

To Sum Up

John and Mary have found that the **tools for thinking** help them meet their life situations with an unusual degree of wisdom and maturity. They see all around them people whose lives are marred by constant bickering and fussing, simply because they have not trained themselves to use these **tools for thinking.** They have read that one out of every three marriages of couples their age breaks up. They believe that few marriages would fail if people were taught to use these **tools for thinking** in their everyday problems.

Effective Thinking in Business

To a scientist a theory is something to be *tested.* He seeks not to defend his beliefs, but to improve them. He is, above everything else, an expert at "changing his mind." *

WENDELL JOHNSON

Our business life, like our personal life, presents a steady stream of problems. Success in business depends upon how well we meet the day-by-day challenges to our thinking ability that come before us. No one has a 100 per cent score in making sound decisions, but it is possible to train ourselves so we will have a pretty high batting average.

By now you should be familiar enough with **so far as I know, up to a point, to me,** and the **what, when,** and **where indexes** to enable you to sense their use in business situations. So instead of going through these tools, one by one, and showing some detailed applications in business, let's see how useful the scientific method can be in solving business problems. I hope

* From *People in Quandaries* by Wendell Johnson. New York: Harper & Brothers. Copyright, 1946. Reprinted by permission.

to convince you that it is impossible to achieve a high average in batting out sound business decisions without the scientific attitude.

As pointed out in Chapter 2, the scientist does not settle things by arguing about them—he decides things by surveying the territory. Facts first, then opinions. He is like that proverbial man from Missouri—you've got to show him. Talking does not convince him—he knows how easy it is to be misled by prejudices and preconceived ideas. Now let us see how the scientific attitude of surveying the territory is a basic necessity in the business world.

He Climbed to the Top

Edward A. Deeds, who rose to chairman of the National Cash Register Company, was first employed by that company at their Dayton, Ohio, factory as a twenty-five-year-old construction and maintenance engineer. One day Deeds noticed an apparent roughness at the top of a 175-foot brick smokestack. He studied it carefully through field glasses and looked up the construction drawings for the smokestack. He decided that heat must have expanded the inner core and was loosening the outside ring of bricks. If this was happening, lives and property were in danger. When he told the factory manager about this, his observations were dismissed with the brusque comment: "That stack was put up by engineers who have put up more chimneys than you have ever seen."

Now what did Deeds do? Did he go to town with a lot of argument and words? Did he try to tell the plant manager that he had made a mistake in judgment?

FACTS SETTLE ARGUMENTS

"Hey, Mac—ROAD MAP!!"

Deeds did none of these things. He set about to survey the territory more carefully so that the facts could speak for themselves. On the following Sunday afternoon when the furnace was off, he put on foundryman-gloves and, with a wet sponge over his nose, climbed up the still hot and sooty interior all the way to the top of the stack.

There he examined the damage that was taking place. He hooked up a suspension rig which enabled him to reach the outside of the stack to study conditions more closely. He outlined the damaged area with chalk and took photographs to show the condition of the stack when relatively cool. To make sure the facts would be sufficiently eloquent to convince the plant manager, he used the suspension rig to go up again on Monday while the stack was hot. The bricks were so loose that he actually brought down a couple with him. The photographs taken on Monday, when compared with those taken on Sunday, showed clearly that the cracks were due to expansion when the stack was hot.

Then Deeds let the bricks and the photographs do the talking. The factory manager apologized and told Deeds warmly: "Whatever you do in this plant hereafter will have my full support."

Edward A. Deeds began his rise to leadership in business by climbing to the top of a hot, sooty smokestack to enable him to base his verbal maps on an adequate survey of the territory. His distinguished career with the National Cash Register Company and in other fields has shown the importance of rounding up the facts needed and *then letting those facts convince people.*

The Scientific Method

The scientific method is a three-step process:

1. You use your imagination and your memory to think up explanations or possible solutions for your problems.
2. You analyze them logically—you try to visualize how each solution will work out. And then you're ready for the third step *without which thinking is not scientific*—
3. You survey the territory. You test your idea by trying it. You let the facts speak for themselves.

Let's follow the experiences of Mr. Plunge and Mr. Checkit to see how this works out in business.

While Mr. Plunge was in the Army, he invented a new kind of can opener and a smooth-working rattrap. And Mr. Checkit during his years in a war factory also did some inventing. He had ideas for a more efficient kitchen knife sharpener and an improved kitchen grater. Both men planned to use their savings to go into business with their inventions.

When the war ended, Mr. Plunge plunged right in. He took a long-term lease (at high postwar rental) on a building that was to be his shop and office. He mortgaged his home to purchase machinery he needed for making his can opener and rattrap in mass production. He used his savings to purchase office equipment and to begin a large newspaper and mail-order campaign. He began to sell quite a number of can openers, but people just did not buy many of the rattraps. By this time, being hard pressed for cash, he decided reluctantly that the rattrap was not much of a money-maker after all, and it would

You use your imagination and your memory to think up explanations or possible solutions to your problem.

You analyze them logically and try to visualize how each solution will work out.

You test your idea by trying it out.

be better to sell the special machines he had bought for making rattraps and use that money in heavier promotion of the can openers. About this time, many of the can openers came back for repair. Quickly he saw that by making two improvements in the design and by using a tougher kind of metal, he could get rid of the causes for complaints. This meant getting another machine which he financed from the rattrap machinery that was sacrificed at half price.

But now the squeeze was on. He needed money to promote sales accounts in other states. This meant putting a second mortgage on his home. "Oh, well," he said, "a guy has to take risks if he wants to get anywhere in business. I've done the best I could. No one is right all the time."

But let us see how Mr. Checkit went about it. He knows that no one is right all the time, and he also knows that you've got to take risks if you want to get anywhere in business. But he thinks a person is a fool to take any greater risk than is necessary. So Mr. Checkit, instead of plunging right in with his bright ideas, tries, whenever possible, to check them in a small way before jumping in in a large way. In short, he uses the scientific method of testing out ideas before endorsing them.

Mr. Checkit knows that when a scientist in a laboratory develops what he thinks is a new cure for some disease, he first tries it on a few guinea pigs. If he gets the results he expects, he continues his tests on a larger scale. After he feels he has tested it as carefully as possible with animals, he is then ready to try it on a few human beings—but not too many. If it works out well with a small group, he makes arrangements to get it tried out with several thousand people. In the scientific

A SINGLE EXTRA FACT CAN CHANGE THE COMPLEXION OF A SITUATION

"Who the hell taught YOU how to drive—"

"—sir."

world, this careful testing process protects us against a lot of half-baked, dangerous, or useless ideas.

Now scientific Mr. Checkit, like unscientific Mr. Plunge, thought that his two inventions would make a nice postwar business for him. But he realizes how easy it is to believe what one wants so earnestly to believe. He knows that no matter how wonderful his knife sharpener and grater are **to him,** *the only important thing is whether other people want them enough to buy them.* And he knows he is no judge of that.

So before spending his savings in machinery and advertising, he paid a small manufacturing company to turn out 200 of each of these inventions. He left some of them at local hardware stores on consignment and also ran a small three-inch advertisement in a farm magazine. Within a week he had 78 mail orders for knife sharpeners, and the hardware stores reported they could use more. But the cheese graters were not selling well. The hardware stores had sold less than a dozen. So he decided to push the knife sharpener and forget about the grater for the time being. But he did not plunge yet. He ordered five hundred more of the knife sharpeners and took them around to more hardware stores, some grocery stores, and a ten-cent store. He wanted to be reasonably sure before he risked all his savings. He wanted to find out if people would find flaws in the knife sharpener, too.

After the rapid sale of the batch of 500, he was fairly sure that he had something people would buy. But fairly sure was not good enough for him. This time he ordered 2500 of them. And he had a better looking box printed to make his product more attractive. When he saw that this

TEST THINGS BEFORE RELYING ON THEM

"And canvas. . . ."

group was selling well, he decided to purchase the machinery he needed to make them himself.

He is now doing a thriving business turning out knife sharpeners and also several other household gadgets. He still thinks his cheese grater is a good idea—but he's not going to throw away a lot of money getting set to make graters until the public shows some signs of agreeing with him. "It's easy to sell myself on *my* ideas," he says, "but the important thing is to make sure that the *public* can be sold on them before I risk my shirt."

Look before You Leap

No matter how smart we are, there are some things that we just cannot figure out. Our knowledge is never complete, and we do not know ALL the factors that will influence what we are doing. And sometimes a single overlooked factor can make the difference between success and failure.

To be successful in the business world, we need to check our bright ideas against the territory. Our enthusiasm must be restrained long enough for us to analyze our ideas critically. Whenever possible, we should not go all-out until we get a chance to test them thoroughly. Do not speak for the facts—make the facts speak for themselves.

John H. Jacobs of the O. P. Baur Confectionery Company of Denver, Colorado, says:

> There is a tendency on the part of business executives to speak first and check facts later. . . . In the past, once our plans were laid we made every effort to prove that *our* thinking was right, and we often attempted to make the facts adjust

"Over ten, is he? Well, you've pulled that once too often, my good man, because it just so happens that I have his birth certificate right here!"

to our planning and thinking. As a result we found ourselves in constant conflict. Today we take a different approach. We make our plans and then continually check them against life-facts. If they do not agree with the facts we adjust our plans accordingly. We have learned the lesson that you cannot adjust outside facts to your own personal *thinking*. You have to adjust your thinking to the facts as they are today and as they constantly change.*

Sometimes, the experience of other people can furnish us with facts we need, but we must remember that **situation$_1$** is not **situation$_2$** and what works or does not work in one place may turn out differently somewhere else—or at another time. We must learn to observe what particular kinds of mistakes in thinking we make most often. Is it from not seeking the advice of others? Or is it from not using adequately our own experiences and our own ideas? Is it from not testing our ideas in a small way before relying upon them in a large way? Each one of us must act as his own judge in finding out his own particular weaknesses in thinking.

In a barrel full of new ideas, there will be, most likely, some good ones and some rotten ones. The problem is: how can we tell the useful ideas from the impractical ones? Our past experience can help us only **up to a point.** Only the scientific method of open-minded testing can enable us to find that profitable path between the marshes of inborn conservatism and the quicksands of plunging optimism.†

* Reprinted by permission of the author and *The Mines Magazine*. Copyright, 1944.

† For an interesting account of the scientific method applied to business, personal, and social problems, read Stuart Chase's *The Proper Study of Mankind*, Harper & Brothers, New York, 1948.

To Sum Up

The scientific attitude is as useful in running a business as in running a scientific laboratory. In both, it is fact, not fancy, that enables us to think straight and find what really works.

The scientific method helps us meet new situations without making fools of ourselves. And **up to a point** every situation in life is a new situation—different in time, different in place, and different in the individuals and things involved. We cannot use the scientific method in making ALL our decisions, but when making our most important ones, we should remember that it is the most useful method known to help us turn up facts we need to make sound decisions *that will apply to present conditions.*

14

The Why and Wherefore

Happy he who could perceive the causes of things.

VIRGIL

When you learn to use the **tools for thinking** in a systematic way, you will be surprised at their versatility. They are useful in practically all your life situations—if you know how to handle them maturely. In this chapter, you will see how the six **tools for thinking** can help you understand the problems you face when making the apparently simple statement, "This is the cause of that."

A large part of our serious thinking (if not most of it) deals with trying to find reliable answers to the question: WHY? As Virgil recognized around two thousand years ago, our success and happiness depend upon how adequately we can answer the WHYS in our lives:

WHY doesn't she love me?

WHY can't I make more money?

WHY don't my hollyhocks grow?

WHY am I not so popular as Bill Jones?
WHY does the roof leak?
WHY doesn't Junior mind me?
WHY is the income-tax rate so high?
WHY must my son go to war?
WHY do I get headaches so often?
—and so on into the night.

Tool No. 1: So Far As I Know

The tool **so far as I know** will remind us that the causes of anything and everything are infinitely complex, and no one has ALL the answers. No matter what we say is "the" reason for something, there are always many other underlying reasons that have been overlooked.

It is impossible to give a complete answer to any WHY. For instance, suppose our car has hiccups and we take it to a mechanic for a diagnosis. His answer to WHY the car is not running smoothly is that the ignition wires are shorting out. But we may ask, "Why are the ignition wires shorting out?"

"They are shorting because the insulation is breaking down."

"Why is the insulation breaking down?"

"The insulation is breaking down because of dampness and heat and other conditions that tend to deteriorate rubber and cotton."

"But why . . . ?"

For an answer to this WHY we might have to go to the microscopic level. But to any answer that is produced, it is possible to ask another WHY. After a few more WHYS, we will be down to the level of molecules and atoms. And if we insist upon asking WHY to every answer, sooner or later we will

THE CAUSES OF ANYTHING AND EVERYTHING ARE INFINITELY COMPLEX, AND NO ONE HAS ALL THE ANSWERS

WHERE DOES THE APPLE COME FROM?

"THE GROCERY STORE."

Ted Key

Where Does the Apple Come From?

come to a point where the best specialist in the world can no longer answer us. His knowledge gives out, and if he is wise he will let his answers do likewise. But, of course, anyone who has been around young children already knows that for every answer, a WHY can be asked.

Fortunately in most of our everyday situations, we do not need complete answers to our WHYS. When the garageman tells us that worn-out ignition cables are "the" cause of the motor's skipping, we usually prefer to go no further into the why and wherefore.

Causes Are Complex

One person said, "To know the complete cause of anything, you would have to know the cause of everything."

Many years ago the price of real estate in the Harlem district of New York City was raised because of changes in the design of some train engines. Here's how it happened:

1. These changes in design allowed a larger firebox.
2. This gave the engine more pulling power.
3. It could then bring longer passenger trains into Grand Central Terminal.
4. More passengers meant more luggage to be carried a longer distance to the street.
5. Then the station needed more Negro porters.
6. Since most of the redcaps lived in one section of Harlem, the landlords were able to raise the rents.
7. When the rents went up, the value of the property went up.

But was the improved firebox of the locomotive the whole answer to WHY the price of Harlem real estate went up? Of course not. There are thousands of other factors that played both large and small parts. "The causes of events," said Cicero, "are more interesting than the events themselves."

Notice how often people habitually say, "*THE* cause of this is that," instead of "*A* cause of this is that." More than half the time you will find that they are naïvely blinded by the habit of saying, "THE cause. . . ." It is surprising how much can depend on whether we use the word "*A*" or "*THE*." "*THE*" implies an "I've-said-the-last-word" attitude. "*A*" leaves the door open.

I know of nothing in this world about which it can be said, "This is THE cause of that, and that's ALL there is to it. There are no underlying factors and no other things that are causally related." Only a **so-far-as-I-know** attitude equips us to find our way in this complex world we live in.

Following After; Therefore Caused By

There is an old story about an American frontiersman who had never had any medical instruction, but who thought he would try his hand at practicing medicine. His first patient was a blacksmith who seemed to be ill with typhoid fever. When the blacksmith asked for some pork and beans, the amateur doctor said it would be all right on the theory that his patient might as well die happily. But the sturdy blacksmith rallied and completely recovered in a few days. Noting these facts, the "doctor" made the following entry in his medical book: "For typhoid fever, prescribe pork and beans."

WHENEVER TWO THINGS HAPPEN CLOSELY TOGETHER THAT ARE NOT CAUSALLY RELATED, WE ARE IN DANGER OF THE "FOLLOWING-AFTER-THEREFORE-CAUSED-BY" FALLACY

The tool **so far as I know** can help us avoid what is known to logic professors as the *Post hoc ergo propter hoc* fallacy: FOLLOWING AFTER; THEREFORE CAUSED BY. We live in a world where appearances are often deceptive. Things do not come neatly labeled "Cause" and "Effect." We have to decide for ourselves when to pin these labels on.

Whenever two things happen closely together that are not causally related, we are in danger of the following-after-therefore-caused-by fallacy. Two moonshiners from the Smoky Mountains were taking their first trip on a train. They had heard of soda pop, but neither had tasted any. So when the vendor came through the car, they each bought a bottle.

The first moonshiner wiped the lip of the bottle on the back of his hand and took a long drink—just as the train entered a tunnel.

"How is it, Snuffy?" asked his friend in the darkness.

"Don't tetch thet stuff, Jed," Snuffy said in a trembling voice. "I been struck blind!"

Practically all our superstitions are due to this following-after-therefore-caused-by fallacy. Sometime someone somewhere broke a mirror and for the next seven years life seemed tougher than usual. Slapping a cause-effect relationship on this, someone generalized that it is seven years' bad luck to break a mirror. There is an interesting superstition that four-leaf clovers will bring good luck. But Mrs. Wilmore Trotter Johnson of Coeburn, Virginia, has found and saved thousands of four-leaf clovers, and she has been in five automobile wrecks, has lost three husbands, and has suffered so many misfortunes she is known as "Calamity Jane."

FOLLOWING-AFTER; THEREFORE-CAUSED-BY

"Uh, uh. Mac's mother-in-law. Betcha there'll be trouble."

"What'd I tell you. Mac's leaving."

"Finally got your suitcase back. Mother-in-law returned it."

The tool **so far as I know** can remind us that we often associate things that have no causal connections. Shortly before the last war ended, an elderly man was taking a bath in his home in London. When he had finished his bath, he reached down to pull the stopper in the tub. Just as the stopper came out, the house exploded. The rescue crew made its way through the debris of the bombed house, and found him still in the tub muttering away to himself, "I just don't understand it. All I did was pull the plug out." *Following after; therefore caused by!*

Whenever we say, "This is the cause of that," we lay ourselves open to the following-after-therefore-caused-by fallacy. Nothing will protect us against it completely. An open mind that is willing to try to understand other points of view and which *tests things when possible* is the only defense against this mistake.

The Unwary Are Misled

Dryden wrote:

> Errors, like straws, upon the surface flow;
> He who would search for pearls must dive below.

Significant causes are like gold. Some of the time they lie on the surface, but frequently they are hidden deeply underneath. For example, suppose we find the town of A-ville has a lot of drinking and poverty in it, and B-ville has very little drinking and poverty. We tend to jump to the conclusion that drinking causes the poverty.

Yet there is nothing whatsoever in these facts that could

CAUSES ARE COMPLEX

"Don't know why I did it—probably don't get enough Vitamin A."

justify such a conclusion. This inference *may be right,* but further investigation is necessary to find out whether drinking causes the poverty, or whether the poverty causes the drinking. Or it may be that other things are responsible for both the drinking and the poverty. It may be that A-ville has poor schools and that ignorance is a common cause of both drinking and poverty. There are hundreds of different things that could cause both of them.

Generally situations are complex and it takes a lot of fact-finding and open-minded thinking to root out significant causes and effects. Many things play a large or small part in everything that happens. We must be wary of verbal maps that oversimplify and distort the picture.

It has been found that the large increase in college enrollment during the past few decades has been accompanied by a rise in the number of people entering insane asylums. Is one of these "the" cause of the other? Probably not. It has been found that there is often a close correspondence between the average salaries of Presbyterian ministers in Massachusetts and the price of rum in Havana, Cuba. Is one of these "the" cause of the other? Probably not. In this wide world of ours, two things can occur together and not be causally connected. We must not allow ourselves to be misled by chance correlation.

Again, the tool **so far as I know** will remind us that the causes of things are usually very complex, and, in important matters, we would do well to dig deeply under the surface to uncover significant causes. And no matter how sure we are of our diagnosis of "THE" cause, we must stay on the lookout for new facts which will allow us to reinterpret old facts and thereby mature our verbal maps.

Tool No. 2: Up to a Point of Probability

If our knowledge were complete, we could say, "This IS" or "This IS NOT a cause." But since we do not know ALL about anything, we can probably never be absolutely sure about causes in a complex situation. We should therefore think in terms of degrees of probability. We should ask ourselves **up to what point** our verbal maps are supported by evidence.

Depending upon the quality and quantity of evidence we have, we should rate our diagnosis of cause in terms of varying degrees of probability. Let us represent different degrees of probability as a series of steps going from high to low degrees of probability:

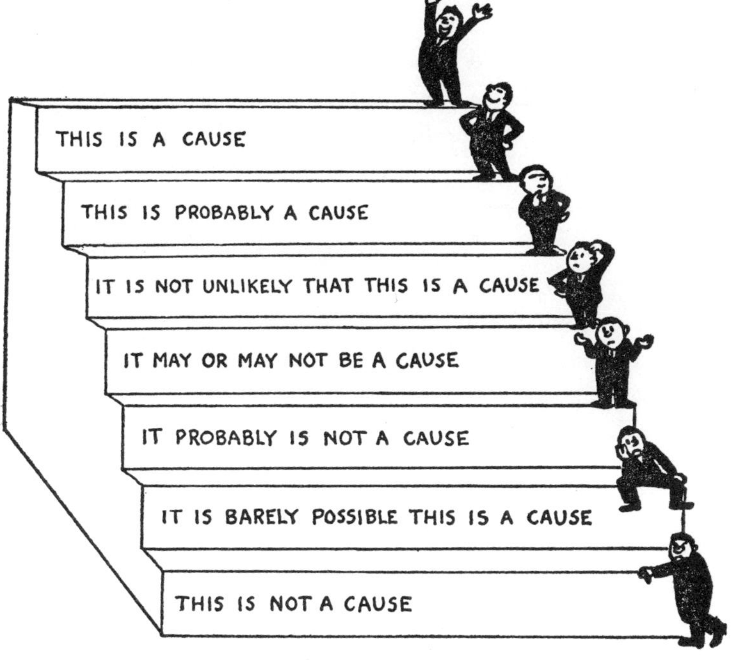

Probability has little to do with truth. Truth refers to the way things are—whatever that is. *Probability refers to the quality and quantity of the evidence that supports our maps.* For example, back in 1400 the verbal map, "The world is round," was a very improbable verbal map. Probability is based on evidence, and the known evidence for that verbal map in 1400 was not sufficiently adequate to establish overwhelmingly the notion that the world was round. Today the verbal map, "The world is round," is highly probable—about as certain as anything we have. The world has not changed its shape a great deal since 1400, *but our evidence about it has.* As our knowledge progressed, the "round world" verbal map became more and more probable even though it contradicts the "flat" earth we see with our own eyes.

No verbal map is probable in itself. It is only *probable because of the evidence that supports it. When the weight of evidence changes, the probability changes.* If we get more evidence to support a map, it becomes more probable. If we find evidence that contradicts it, it becomes less probable. Since our evidence is never complete, we must watch for new facts that will raise or lower the probability of our verbal maps. The tool **up to a point** can help us think in terms of probability. It can remind us to make degree maps to fit the degree nature of our knowledge.

Tool No. 3: To Me

Our interests and point of view determine to a large extent what causal factors we consider important. What may be an important cause **to us** may not be important **to someone else.** We must not fool ourselves into thinking that we see only the

TO GET PEOPLE TO UNDERSTAND OUR POINT OF VIEW, WE MUST FIRST TRY TO UNDERSTAND THEIRS

"Eighty cents a pound. I just can't understand *why* she won't eat it."

"true" causes of things. *We see the causes we are hunting for, and we reject as insignificant the causes that do not embrace our interests.*

Dr. H. A. Larrabee tells of a news story in *The New York Times* headed "Income Tax Leads to Fire." Edward J. Reynolds, a forty-six-year-old accountant, had worked through the night trying to get his income-tax return completed. He dozed off about 5:45 A.M. and his lighted cigarette fell on an overstuffed chair beside his desk. A fire started and the smoke fumes knocked him out. Neighbors observed the smoke. The firemen came quickly and put out the blaze. There was about $400 damage.

If you ask the Chief of the Tarrytown Fire Department what was "the" cause of the fire, he would reply, "Carelessness." If you ask the physician who attended Mr. Reynolds about "the" cause of the fire, he would say, "Fatigue and drowsiness caused by overwork." The newspaperman who reported the incident had interests that led him to see still another cause for the fire. He was interested in the conditions that led Mr. Reynolds to work out complicated income-tax returns requiring the all-night stint. So, **to the reporter,** the cause of the fire was that darn income-tax form. Each of these three people had different interests and reactions which led them to three different conclusions.

What was really "the" cause of the fire? Was it carelessness or fatigue and drowsiness? Or was it actually the complicated income-tax form? These are nonsense questions. There is no such thing as "THE" cause. For everything that happens there are many underlying causal factors. Every person will single

OUR MINDS SELECT THE CAUSES
THAT FIT IN WITH OUR PERSONAL INTERESTS

"That's not the way I heard it."

out as most important the one that his own interests and knowledge pick out for him.

The above discussion of the causes of this fire by no means exhausts the possibilities. They only represent "the" cause from the point of view of **fire chief$_1$**, **doctor$_1$**, and **reporter$_1$**. Suppose you ask a coffee salesman what "the" cause was. He would tell you it was Mr. Reynolds' failure to drink a few cups of coffee (his brand). If you ask a metal furniture representative about "the" cause, he might reply that it was because people insist on sticking to old-fashioned overstuffed furniture. If you ask an anticigarette leaguer about "the" cause, she might point out "the smoking habit is to blame."

For the prevention of further accidents of this kind, some points of view may be more useful than others. But all points of view are useful in helping us build up the fullest understanding of what happened and why. We must avoid the temptation to play favorites and to insist that any one point of view is "THE" cause.

So, whenever we start talking about "the" cause of something, we should be sure to add **to me** to our verbal maps to remind us that we are diagnosing causes from OUR OWN point of view, and that there are many other possible points of view besides ours. **To me** reminds us that the causes WE pick out are significant **to us** because of our own personal interests and the way we were born and bred.

Tools 4, 5, and 6: The What, When, and Where Indexes

In our search for causes, the **indexes** remind us to avoid being fooled by differences: differences in individuals, differences in time, and differences in places. By making us more sensitive

OUR WHYS AND WHEREFORES MAY CHANGE WITH THE TIMES

". . . then why have sales dropped? We turn out the best candle snuffers in the world!"

to differences, the **indexes** help us adapt our past experiences to new people and things, new times and new places. As Winston Churchill observed in his *Memoirs* when commenting on the "Maginot Line" thinking of the French military leaders, "Past experience carries with its advantages the drawback that things never happen the same way again."

To make room for the extended discussion of the **so far as I know** tool in the first part of this chapter, it has been necessary to omit examples illustrating the **what, when, and where indexes.** How about thinking up some good examples for yourself?

To Sum Up

The causes of things are often complex and slippery, and even the most brilliant thinkers can be misled. The **tools for thinking** will do a great deal to help us understand some of the problems we face whenever we are bull-headed enough to state: "This is THE cause of that."

The tool **so far as I know** reminds us that every effect is brought about by countless preceding factors about which our knowledge is incomplete. **Up to a point** reminds us that our maps will have varying degrees of probability depending on **up to what point** they are supported by facts. The more evidence we have, the greater the probability. When contradicting evidence is found, the degree of probability drops fast. **To me** will remind us that we pick out causes in which we are interested and ignore other aspects that are perhaps just as important. When we claim, "**To me** this is the most important cause," we leave the door open to consider other points of view. The **what index** tells us that no two situations are exactly alike in all respects. The **when index** will remind us that we cannot rely blindly on our former experiences because the causes of things may change from time to time. The **where index** alerts us to the possibility that a different environment may bring different results.

15

Thinking for Tomorrow

The future of democracy is allied with the spread of the scientific attitude. It is the sole guarantee against wholesale misleading by propaganda. More important still, it is the only assurance of the possibility of a public opinion intelligent enough to meet present social problems.

JOHN DEWEY

The famous psychologist, Dr. Edward L. Thorndike, has compared the animal-like ways we settle disagreements between nations with the apparently more human methods used by the howler monkeys. Most of the time each nation of monkeys stays in its own territory and minds its own business. But when a group of monkeys trespasses on the territory of another group, they are immediately met with a vigorous chorus of howls. The invaders reply by howling back.

> The contest continues until, by a beneficent provision in the brain of the howler monkey, the side that is outhowled is moved to retire. Not a drop of blood is spilled; not an atom of

"Here's that ferocious killer I was telling you about."

food or shelter is destroyed. No blot stains the national honor, since each citizen howls its loudest until its inner nature says, "Howled enough!". . . . The outcomes are surely far better than in man where the large wins over the small, the bellicose over the peaceful, and force over reason.

Thinking: By the People, Not for the People

The *people* of a country have nothing to gain by an aggressive war. But their minds are so drugged with lies and so stimulated by appeals to patriotism that they willingly cooperate with the unscrupulous leaders who plan wars for their own private ends. Until the *people* of a country learn to compare the statements of their political leaders with the territory those statements are supposed to represent, and arrive at their own conclusions and act on them, that long will the people of more than 100 countries of this world be lured into wars in which they have nothing to gain and almost everything to lose.

Dr. G. M. Gilbert, who served as Prison Psychologist at the Nuremberg trials of the Nazi war criminals, reports what Hermann Goering told him in his cell in reply to a question about the people's attitude toward war:

> "Why, of course, the *people* don't want war," Goering shrugged. "Why should . . . [someone] want to risk his life in a war when the best he can get out of it is to come back . . . in one piece. Naturally, the common people don't want war; neither in Russia nor in England nor in America, nor, for that matter, in Germany. That is understood. But after all, it is the *leaders* of the country who determine the policy and it is always a simple matter to drag the people along, whether it is a democracy or a fascist dictatorship or a parliament or a Com-

IT BEGAN WITH A CLUB

One club—1 dead

One cannon—8 dead

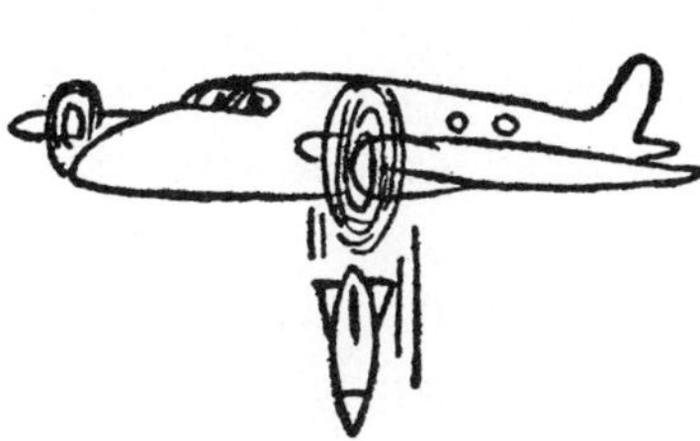

One bomb—80 dead

One torpedo—800 dead

One atomic bomb—80,000 dead

One H bomb—8,000,000 dead?

WHEN WILL IT END?

munist dictatorship . . . Voice or no voice, the people can always be brought to the bidding of the leaders. That is easy. All you have to do is tell them they are being attacked and denounce the pacifists for lack of patriotism and exposing the country to danger. It works the same in any country." *

One Hundred Children

During the time it takes you to read this chapter, about one hundred children will be born in the United States. What thinking habits will they pick up? Or let me put the question in another way: If we wanted to do the worst possible job of teaching young children to think, what habits would we give them? What could we do to make sure that they would be unable to think for themselves? How could we train young children so that the political leaders in their country would have as little trouble as possible in "dragging them along"? How could we make them such slaves to words that facts would have little effect on them? How can we twist their young minds so as to make them as dogmatic, frustrated, and unhappy as possible?

To begin with, we would have to teach these young children to act as though their maps represented ALL of the territory. At all costs, we must prevent them from achieving an "I-don't-know-all-let's-see" attitude. And they must regard even the slightest criticism as an unfriendly provocation.

These little children must not think in terms of a process world. And they must not try to keep their verbal maps up to date. They must be made to feel that changing one of their verbal maps means a mortal blow to their pride and ego.

* From *Nuremberg Diary* by G. M. Gilbert. New York: Farrar, Straus & Co., Inc. Reprinted by permission.

We must teach them to prove their points by quoting authorities—the more ancient the better. We must somehow, but subtly, put across the notion that they are not to do their own thinking. Their thinking must be confined to finding good reasons to continue believing what they have been taught. They must treat their ideas, *not as maps, but as if they were exact copies of the territory.* They must believe implicitly that their words do not *represent* the territory: they ARE the territory!

They must insist on making sweeping statements about groups and refuse to look at **man**$_1$ or **thing**$_1$. They must have the EITHER-OR habit of thinking and never think in terms of degrees. They must claim that logical consistency demands that things be either ALL-or-NONE.

If we were trying to give little children the thinking habits that would make their lives as difficult as possible, we must teach them to judge all people by their own reactions and view as fools those who do not agree with them. When they say **"to me,"** they must mean, "to all intelligent and sensible people." They must be trained to have quick and undelayed reactions, and they must never retract a snap judgment any more than an umpire changes the way he calls a ball.

Above all, it will be necessary for them to avoid the scientific method of thinking. They must believe that their maps are more important than the territory, and to test them by actually trying them out would be quite unnecessary. In short, they must keep their eyes and minds closed.

Actually, I don't know any children in this country who have been trained with the above objectives in view. But read over this list again. See if you do not find that you tend to have some of the above thinking habits. I find I do. Look at the people around you. How many of them have these immature thinking habits?

The Failure of the Schools

"The great end of education," said Tryon Edwards, "is to discipline rather than to furnish the mind; to train it to the use of its own powers, rather than fill it with the accumulations of others."

At the present time most schools do little to equip children with mature thinking habits. They cram into them all sorts of knowledge (some useful—some useless), but the children are given precious few hints on how to weed out false knowledge and keep the rest in good repair. Little Dickie expressed the attitude of far too many children one day in his geography class:

Teacher: "Richard, give me three proofs that the world is round."

Dickie: "First, you say so; second, Daddy says so; and third, the book says so."

"It is hardly an exaggeration," said John Dewey, "to say that too often the pupil is treated as if he were a phonographic record on which is impressed a set of words that are to be literally reproduced when the recitation or examination presses the proper lever. Or, varying the metaphor, the mind of the pupil is treated as if it were a cistern into which information is conducted by one set of pipes that mechanically pour it in, while the recitation is the pump that brings out the material again through another set of pipes. Then the skill of the teacher

CHILDREN PICK UP THE HABITS OF THOSE AROUND THEM

"Don't try to tell *me* what's right! I've lived a lot longer than you, young man!"

is rated by his or her ability in managing the two pipe-lines of flow inward and outward."*

In short, the schools put their efforts into teaching children WHAT TO THINK and fail in the more important thing—teaching them HOW TO THINK. Nothing in education is more important—yet nothing is more neglected.

As the Twig Is Bent

In the more than 100 countries of this world, in the thousands of cities and villages on this globe, little children are being indoctrinated with whatever sense and nonsense their elders desire. Experience has shown that there is almost no limit to the absurdities little children can swallow. "We begin," says Bain, "by believing everything." Children who are taught WHAT TO THINK but not HOW TO THINK can only repeat the errors men have been making for centuries. Instead of maturely evaluating their verbal maps and the maps of other people, they can only fight about them. All of us have had the experience of hearing the words, "It ain't so," followed by a solid whack of fist against flesh. This in microcosm is a pattern of war.

General G. Brock Chisholm, Executive Secretary of the United Nations' World Health Organization, warns: "The world is changing and will continue to change so quickly that it is impossible for us to give clear-cut and definite plans for living to our children. It is impossible for us to present them with maps of reality with any degree of belief that these maps

* From *How We Think* by John Dewey. Reprinted by special permission of D. C. Heath and Company, Boston, Mass.

will continue to have validity after the passage of twenty or thirty years. What children need from their parents is not maps of the world as it used to be, nor of the beliefs of their parents or their ancestors, but the great gift of freedom to think, ability themselves to look clearly at reality and to make up their own minds how best to arrange their own relationships with the reality they see clearly." *

How should we teach our children? How can we pass along the valuable experiences and great traditions of the past and at the same time encourage the coming generation to adapt them to the world of tomorrow?

My wife and I are teaching our children the "right" and "wrong" as we see it. They are going to start out with the opinions we have. We feel that we must give them a set of morals; that we must give them a set of ideas on how to get along in the world; that we must introduce them to our "friends" and "foes." But we do not feel it is right *to make them carry on* our friendships or our feuds. Our children are learning to use the **tools for thinking.**† We are teaching them that our ideas are the best ones we have been able to find thus far. But they are also learning that it is up to them to mature the ideas they have received from us so they can pass them on in better form to their children.

We are placing upon them the burden and obligation to mature and change the ideas they have been taught when they find those ideas do not adequately fit *their* life facts. Instead of

* Reprinted with the kind permission of G. Brock Chisholm and *The Christian Register*.

† If you would like to see how easily the tools for thinking can be presented to a child, see page 239.

trying to turn out mimics who will feel guilty if they ever disagree with us, we challenge our children to survey the territory for themselves and work out for themselves better verbal maps than we have been able to give them. They should no more revere and treasure the verbal maps they inherit than the family car they fall heir to. When better cars are available, they will want to get one. When more adequate verbal maps are produced, they had better get those too.

We openly confess to our children that Daddy and Mommy do not know ALL about EVERYTHING. We say to them: "We've had a lot more experience than you and we believe at the present time you will find that our verbal maps have, on the whole, pretty good predictability. But in this rolling world, the circumstances vary. As you grow up, you've got to begin to do your own thinking."

Here is how Lincoln Steffens taught his son:

> A faucet is out of order. It leaks and I cannot close it tight. Good. I call my seven-year-old son to look it over and take another lesson in one of the most important courses I have to teach him. He seizes the faucet, tries to turn it off, can't. He grins.
>
> "What's the matter, Pete?" I ask.
>
> He looks up happily, and gives the answer. "Grown-ups, Daddy."
>
> Propaganda, of course. I have taught him that we, his elders, cannot make a fit faucet. And he may. There's a job for him and his generation in the plumbing business. And in every other business.
>
> I teach my child and, as I get the chance, I tell all the other children of all ages—pre-school, in school, in college, and out:

IF WE FAIL. . . .

"Oops!! Not there!! Still radioactive!!"

That nothing is done, finally and right.

That nothing is known, positively and completely.

That the world is theirs, all of it. It is full of jobs for them, full of all sorts of things for them to find out and do, or do over and do right. And they eat up the good news. They are glad, as I am, that there is something left for them to discover and say and think and do. Something? There is *everything* for youth to take over, and it is an inspiration to them when I confess for all grownups:

That we have not now and never have had in the history of the world a good government.

That there is not now and never has been a perfectly run railroad, school, newspaper, bank, theater, steel mill, factory, grocery store; that no business is or ever has been built, managed, financed, as it should be, must be and will be, some day —possibly in their day.

That what is true of business and politics is gloriously true of the professions, the arts and crafts, the sciences, the sports. That the best picture has not yet been painted; the greatest poem is still unsung; the mightiest novel remains to be written; the divinest music has not been conceived even by Bach. In science, probably ninety-nine percent of the knowable has to be discovered.*

To solve the world's problems, we must have brave new thinkers for our world. Ignorance, prejudice, and the closed mind are feeble remedies for our ills. We must heed the famous warning of Abraham Lincoln, "The dogmas of the quiet past are inadequate to the stormy present. The occasion is piled high with difficulty, and we must rise with the occasion. As our case is new, so we must think anew and act anew."

*From *Lincoln Steffens Speaking*. New York: Harcourt, Brace and Company, Inc. Copyright, 1936. Reprinted by permission.

"Biggest thing, they say, since the H bomb."

The Road Ahead

As long as we continue to cripple the intelligence of our children by not teaching them how to think, we should expect to have recurrent wars, poverty, crime, and other ills. This business of teaching children throughout the world to think clearly so they may settle their disagreements by mature discussion instead of the chain reaction of uranium is not something that can be done in a day or a week or a year. It is something we must work toward. It will take a long time, but the only way to get it done is to begin doing it. We must formulate our ideals. We must explain them to other people. And we must let no opportunities pass for teaching our children to SEE more clearly, THINK more maturely, and FEEL more deeply.

Civilization is just a slow process of learning how to be kind. We must remember with Voltaire that "men will continue to commit atrocities as long as they continue to believe absurdities." And they will continue to believe absurdities until they are taught HOW TO THINK—and not just pumped full of the local ideas of WHAT TO THINK.

Teaching children to think straight is not the complete answer to the world's ills, *but it is an indispensable starting point.* As long as we pipe into the heads of children WHAT TO THINK and fail to train them HOW TO THINK, that long will we have various brands of hell on earth. *This is the challenge of today.* Can we meet it? It is up to us. It is up to YOU and it is up to ME.

To Sum Up

This world needs thinkers—not parrots.

APPENDIX I

Teaching Children the Tools for Thinking

Even children at the grammar-school level can learn to use the **tools for thinking.** The **tools for thinking** can easily be illustrated with as simple a thing as a flower. For example:

Tool No. 1—So Far As I Know: A child can see that it is impossible to know absolutely everything about a flower: how and why it grows, what all the parts look like when greatly magnified, the chemical and physical changes that take place, etc. **So far as I know** must be added to our verbal maps to remind us of things that have been overlooked

Tool No. 2—Up to a Point: All characteristics are to be found in varying degrees: beautiful—ugly, tall—short, large—small, colorful—drab, fragrant—nonfragrant, quick flowering—slow flowering, sun loving—shade loving, etc. All are to be found in different stages—**up to different points.** A given flower will have more or less of these characteristics when compared with other flowers.

Tool No. 3—To Me: No flower means the same to all people. **To some people,** the fragrance is most esteemed; **to others,** the beautiful colors are most appreciated. Tell the child to ask a dozen people why they like a gladiola or a rose. He will find many **to me's.**

Tool No. 4—The What Index: Play a game with the child. Challenge him to find two flowers that are exactly alike. He will prove to himself that he can find two similar flowers but never ones that are exactly alike. **Flower_1** IS NOT **flower_2.**

Tool No. 5—The When Index: You can point out how the flower changes. From a bud it slowly opens its petals. The blossom matures and then dies leaving seeds—and so on through many changes showing that: **flower_1**(*today*) is different from **flower_1**(*tomorrow*).

Tool No. 6—The Where Index: Where the flower is kept has a lot to do with how long it will remain fresh. A **flower**(*on a bush*) will act differently from the same **flower**(*in a vase*). The former keeps its beauty longer. And **flower_1**(*in a vase on a table*) will live longer than **flower_1**(*in a vase near a heater*). We need the **where index** to remind us of environmental factors that make our flower act in different ways.

The **tools for thinking** are vitamins that make for mental growth. Without these mental vitamins, no child can be expected to achieve his greatest intellectual growth.

APPENDIX II

For Further Study

This book presents what to me is only an ABC of straight thinking. The subject has its DEF and XYZ, too, all of which will help you train yourself to get top performance from your mind. You will find that this book has given you a background which will enable you to get pleasure and profit from the following:

Chisholm, Francis P., *Introductory Lectures in General Semantics*, Institute of General Semantics, Lakeville, Conn., 1945.

ETC.: A Review of General Semantics. A quarterly publication. (Published by the International Society for General Semantics, 539 W. North, Chicago 10, Ill.)

Hayakawa, S. I., *Language in Thought and Action*, Harcourt, Brace and Company, Inc., New York, 1949.

Holmes, Roger W., *The Rhyme of Reason*, Appleton-Century-Crofts, Inc., New York, 1941.

Johnson, Wendell, *People in Quandaries*, Harper & Brothers, New York, 1946.

Kraines and Thetford, *Managing Your Mind*, The Macmillan Company, New York, 1946.

Lee, Irving J., *Language Habits in Human Affairs*, Harper & Brothers, New York, 1941.

Mander, A. E., *Logic for the Millions,* Philosophical Library, Inc., New York, 1947.

Rapoport, Anatol, *Science and the Goals of Man,* Harper & Brothers, New York, 1950.

Reilly, William J., *The Twelve Rules for Straight Thinking,* Harper & Brothers, New York, 1947.

Thouless, Robert H., *How To Think Straight,* Simon & Schuster, Inc., New York, 1941.

The following books are more advanced and should be read after studying several of the above-listed works:

Cohen and Nagel, *An Introduction to Logic and Scientific Method,* Harcourt, Brace and Company, Inc., New York, 1934.

George, William H., *The Scientist in Action: A Scientific Study of His Methods,* Emerson Books, Inc., New York, 1938.

Korzybski, Alfred, *Science and Sanity: An Introduction to Non-Aristotelian Systems and General Semantics.* International Non-Aristotelian Library Publishing Company, 3d ed., 1948. (May be obtained from the Institute of General Semantics, Lakeville, Conn.)

Larrabee, Harold A., *Reliable Knowledge,* Houghton Mifflin Company, Boston, 1945.

Index

W

Y